MW00678005

Glowing endorsements for *Bill Keller*

Just The Basics A Guide for the New Shooter is a must read for all shooters. Bill has a way of addressing the complex issue of shooting a gun and presenting the material in a very practical and usable manner. New shooters, in particular, will benefit from Bill's no nonsense writing style. There is more to being a gun owner than simply buying a gun, but unfortunately, for many of us new shooters the learning process can be overwhelming. This book takes the confusion out of the equation. It is a well written, easy to understand, comprehensive collection of years of knowledge and experience.

—Shelby McKenzie
NRA trainer and author of
A Girl and Her Gun gun blog.

"Bill Keller brings his many years of experience with firearms to print in *Just The Basics A Guide for the New Shooter*. There are countless publications out there that attempt to address various aspects of self-defense and defensive shooting, but few of them are truly designed for the person who, for whatever reason, just recently decided to become an armed citizen and start taking personal responsibility for his or her own safety. This book addresses the topic of defensive shooting with the idea of the reader actually learning and developing a skillset from the ground up. Throughout, Bill places a very strong emphasis on safety as well as providing the reader with a logical and well thought out order of progression. I would urge anyone new to gun ownership or defensive shooting to take the time to read this book."

—Chris Shoffner Defensive Shooting Instructor and
NRA Training Counselor Armed Missouri, Inc.

Acknowledgements

I'd like to acknowledge my wife and her willingness to provide me encouragement, give me time to sit and write, and to love me over our 42 years of marriage. Thanks kid! I love you with all my heart.

I'd like to also acknowledge the trainers that have entered my life over the years:

Uncle Ted – the first man to put a gun in my hand as he stood over my shoulder and grumbled "Just pull the damn trigger!" I miss him.

For "Tiny" – the Taiwanese MP who first introduced a young airman to large caliber handguns with his very own WWII vintage 1911.

And finally I'd like to acknowledge Randy, Darin and Jim – some of the best NRA Training Counselors out there today.

Just the Basics
A Guide for the
New Shooter

Bill
Keller

Published by White Feather Press. (www.whitefeatherpress.com)

ISBN 978-1-61808-089-9

Printed in the United States of America

Cover design created by Ron Bell of AdVision Design Group
(www.advisiondesigngroup.com)

White Feather Press

Reaffirming Faith in God, Family, and Country!

Dedication

This book is dedicated to the "new and inexperienced" shooter. You have chosen to begin a path that will enable you to defend yourself, your family and your friends. It's a path that will allow you to put food on the table as well as provide you a broad range of shooting sports – from trap shooting to pistol competitions. You are why instructors learn their craft, hone their skills and spend their energies training new shooters.

This book is dedicated to you.

CONTENTS

Introduction

Personal Defense and the rise of various shooting sports have led to an explosion in the sales of a wide range of firearms. From the most powerful rifle to the smallest of handguns, sales are booming.

There have also been broad changes in our laws – both at the state and federal levels – to reinforce our citizen's rights under the Second Amendment to keep and bear arms. These have led to a much wider ownership of firearms and a significant increase in the number of armed citizens walking our streets each and every day.

In some cases, the rush to purchase and carry a handgun has exceeded the skill set necessary to use the handgun that is carried on the hip or in the pocket or in the handbag. Don't get me wrong, I don't believe laws should be strengthened to support some government official's opinion of what a trained shooter should be – our right to keep and bear arms is already written in stone as far as I'm concerned.

What I do mean is that, as shooters, we need to take our craft seriously. Every craft, every occupation, every hobby has, at its core, a foundation of knowledge that must be known to fully embrace that craft. The shooting sports – and my own personal focus – personal defense, have this foundation as well. My term for them is: Just the Basics. The basics are a core set of knowledge I believe everyone who uses firearms as weapons for the defense of themselves, their family and those around them must know. They describe where we have come from, explain what our tools are, create a common vocabulary that allows us to communicate clearly, provide direction, and help us train and help us grow in our craft.

That is the purpose of this book. I want to introduce you to my core set of *Just the Basics*, to shore up your skill set and to give you tools to take your handgun skills far beyond *Just the Basics*.

Double-action revolver
Single-action revolver

Lands & grooves
6 hour (Swiss)

Semi-auto- Barretta
(double   ?) European made] de cocker
   action ?)   ---
                                       ?

Store immo- Cool dry place
   too much oil not good for gun.

Mey Kecseti
Fred Llubere

CHAPTER 1 – SAFETY

FIREARMS OFFER A UNIQUE SET OF DANGERS that can easily wound or kill. Over years of training and use – both on the range and in the field – a core of safety rules and equipment has evolved. As a new or inexperienced shooter, you have an obligation to learn these rules and integrate them into your use of your firearms. They have been developed to protect you and those around you. Shooters who ignore safety rules are typically those who find themselves with an extra hole in their body or a dead or wounded friend. Learning to properly use a firearm is deadly serious . . . pay attention.

Along with rules to protect you, shooters have also developed equipment to protect their eyes from damage should a firearm have an unexpected catastrophic failure and to protect their ears from the excessively loud noise that accompanies the discharge of a firearm. Again, the shooter who ignores these safety items tempts fate . . . don't be that guy or gal.

A cautious selection of where you shoot goes a long way to help insure your safety. Wide open, unsupervised shooting ranges have a tendency to turn into scenes from the Wild West. Supervised ranges that provide training, security and Range Safety Officers will go a long ways towards insuring your range trips are safe as well as productive.

There are items you will want with you on every range trip. Many of these items revolve around your safety while others revolve around the maintenance of your firearm. A well-equipped range bag can do a lot to make sure you have a safe, fun and productive range trip.

Finally, YOU hold the ultimate responsibility for your safety. Trust no one. Period.

TWO SETS OF RULES

As a new shooter enters the world of firearms training, the very first topic that will be covered is firearms safety. Learning to properly use a firearm, whether for a shooting sport or for personal defense, is a deadly serious process. There is always an opportunity for a simple mistake with deadly consequences.

Trainers and training organizations have established a common core of rules to reduce the possibility of a new shooter leaving the range (or a defensive engagement) with an extra hole or two. These rules fall into two broad categories:

- Rules for the Shooting Sports

- Rules for the Defensive (and Offensive) Use of a Weapon.

Rules for the Shooting Sports

I will define shooting sports as including the various types of target shooting as well as hunting. The Gold Standard when it comes to safety rules for the shooting sports is the NRA – National Rifle Association. They have been conducting firearms training since 1871, and they have developed three simple and concise rules for firearms safety:

1. ALWAYS keep the gun pointed in a safe direction.
2. ALWAYS keep your finger off the trigger until ready to shoot.
3. ALWAYS keep your gun unloaded until ready to use.

ALWAYS keep the gun pointed in a safe direction. A safe direction means a direction in which – even should you accidently discharge your gun – the possibility of fatally injuring someone or doing large scale damage is minimal. On an outdoor shooting range this direction is typically down range (towards the target area) or at the berms that usually surround the range. At an indoor shooting range this direction is typically limited to down range.

In your home, all guns for shooting sports would typically be unloaded and stored in a locked gun vault of some kind. Still, even when handling a gun for cleaning, inspection or repair, care needs to be taken to continue to follow Rule 1 and always keep the gun pointed in a safe direction. The work area you use should be oriented in such a way that when you are working with your gun the barrel points in a safe direction to insure no people are ever in the line of fire.

This rule – this habit – is the single most important trait to develop when you first begin to handle a firearm.

ALWAYS keep your finger off the trigger until ready to shoot. Your trigger finger should be thought of as a separate appendage. Its ONLY purpose is to press the trigger. It is NOT part of the grip of the gun. It is NOT part of the mechanics of the hand used to draw your gun from a holster or mount a rifle or shotgun to your shoulder. Its ONLY PURPOSE is to press the trigger. And a shooter presses the trigger only after proper sight alignment and a proper sight picture have been established.

ALWAYS keep your gun unloaded until ready to shoot. Shooting ranges are usually cold, meaning you do not load your gun until you are on the firing line or in the shooting box. Should your gun have a detachable magazine, it's okay to load the magazine away from the firing line. But, never insert the magazine into the gun until you are on the firing line or in the shooting box.

Most NRA instructors will add a fourth safety rule:

ALWAYS be sure of your target and what's in front of – and behind – it. Just because you are on a designated shooting range, or in a known area for your hunt, you simply cannot depend on your line of fire being clear of people or unintended targets. You MUST be certain you have clearly identified your target and the area between you and the target is clear. And, you must be certain that in the event you miss your target, the area behind your target is clear as well.

These three NRA rules and the typically added fourth are at work every day keeping shooters on the range and in the field safe. But, they are only as effective as you – the shooter – make them. It is YOUR responsibility to follow them each and every time you have a gun in your hand.

Rules for the Defensive (and Offensive) Use of a Weapon

Once you enter the world of the defensive and offensive use of a weapon, the whole thought of rules gives way to mindset. Your weapon has been fully integrated into your life. If you are an armed citizen who has chosen to carry for personal protection, your weapon is on your person the vast majority of the time. Situational awareness has become habit as you walk throughout your day. You carry a tool and evaluate your environment continually. The rules become ways of being ... ways of thinking.

Perhaps the best known list of ways to conduct yourself when carrying a weapon for defensive or offensive purposes was penned by Lt. Col. Jeff Cooper:

    1.   ALL GUNS ARE ALWAYS LOADED.

2.   NEVER LET THE MUZZLE COVER ANYTHING YOU ARE NOT WILLING TO DESTROY.

3.   KEEP YOUR FINGER OFF THE TRIGGER UNTIL YOUR SIGHTS ARE ON THE TARGET.

4.   BE SURE OF YOUR TARGET AND WHAT IS BEHIND IT.

Once you cross into the arena where your gun is used for defensive – or offensive – purposes, you will notice that the tone changes. The word "gun" is typically replaced by "weapon." This is done to make it perfectly clear that you have a deadly weapon in your hand and that in this environment its purpose is to inflict harm on another person – either to stop the threat in most defensive situations or to take a life in an offensive situation. Few shooters outside of law enforcement and the military ever experience the need to take offensive action.

1. ALL GUNS ARE ALWAYS LOADED. If you treat every weapon as if it's loaded, it's less likely you'll do something stupid with it. This also encourages you to develop the habit that should you be handed a weapon you will immediately check to make sure the weapon is unloaded and safe to handle. If you are picking up a weapon with the intent to holster it, it helps insure you will double check that the weapon is properly loaded and all safeties are engaged.

2. NEVER LET THE MUZZLE COVER ANYTHING YOU ARE NOT WILLING TO DESTROY. A weapon is a means of destruction. When you point the barrel of your weapon at a person, it means you are willing to kill that person. Take a moment to think about that statement. While being able to tell your friends "Yes, I carry." what that truly means is that should the situation arise where you will need to actually draw your weapon and use it to protect yourself, your family or your friends – you may actually have to kill someone. There is never any reason whatsoever to point a loaded weapon at anyone unless you are under direct threat and unless you are actually ready to follow through and stop the threat with deadly force.

<u>Important</u>

Firearms laws and the legal justification of using deadly force vary from jurisdiction to jurisdiction. It is strongly recommended you consult a competent, licensed legal expert for the laws in your area.

3. KEEP YOUR FINGER OFF THE TRIGGER UNTIL YOUR SIGHTS ARE ON THE TARGET. There are two elements to aiming a weapon: Sight Alignment and Sight Picture. Sight Alignment means that the front sight is properly aligned with the rear sight. Sight Picture means that these aligned sights (or red dot or scope reticle) are resting on the target you intend to destroy. Until this is accomplished, keep your finger OFF THE TRIGGER. In fact, rather than just keeping your finger straight and outside of the trigger guard, make an effort to raise it up well above the trigger guard so there is no doubt at all that your finger is off the trigger.

4. BE SURE OF YOUR TARGET. At the time of this writing, the Vice President of the United States gave some advice to people who were trying to defend themselves during a home invasion. He simply said that if you were afraid someone was trying to break into your home through your door, to just fire a couple of rounds from a shotgun through to door to stop them. I simply cannot imagine worse advice. In most areas of the country, it is blatantly criminal advice. You, as the shooter, are responsible for each and every round you fire from your weapon, regardless of what your intent was. If you are in fear of your life being lost, and you find it necessary to discharge your weapon at the threat – you MUST BE SURE OF YOUR TARGET! As the shooter, you must always be sure of what is behind your target in the event your round over-penetrates or you miss your shot.

Two different worlds – the world of shooting sports and the world of defensive and offensive shooting. Yet both sets of safety rules get us to the same place – safe shooters who aim only at and press the trigger to shoot only their intended targets. As a shooter, these rules should be part of your life, part of your soul. You, and only you, are responsible for the safe and proper use of your firearm or weapon. You, and only you, are responsible for each and every round that leaves the muzzle of your firearm or weapon.

The safe use of a firearm or weapon is serious business … treat it that way.

Lives depend on it. YOUR life depends on it!

Let me share a personal example of following Rule 4 from my youth while hunting with my Uncle Victor. Quickly – a review of the first three NRA rules of firearm safety:

1: <u>ALWAYS</u> keep your firearm pointed in a safe direction.

2: <u>ALWAYS</u> keep your finger off the trigger until you're ready to shoot.

3: <u>ALWAYS</u> keep your firearm unloaded until you're ready to use it.

Now, on to Rule 4:

4. ALWAYS BE SURE OF YOUR TARGET AND WHAT'S IN FRONT OF – AND BEHIND – IT.

Shooters harp on these rules constantly – real shooters, anyway. I have seen people who seems oblivious to any firearm safety rules whatsoever, but in the community I move in, that is a rarity. And, most shooters will gently – but firmly – remind you if any of the rules are broken. I appreciate that; it works to keep our sport and training much safer.

However, once off the range and in the field, things can go south quickly. In the time it takes to press the trigger that last little 1/64th of an inch, an afternoon's enjoyment can teeter on the edge of disaster.

It was a very warm October afternoon in the early sixties. My cousin Mike had just been presented with a new single-shot .410 shotgun by my Uncle Victor (it was always Victor, never Vic). They were home, visiting my Mom and Grandmother, Uncle Victor's family, as well, and enjoying the early days of hunting season in eastern Michigan.

We had spent an energetic morning walking the fields (sans dog, BTW) and had not really seen much of interest. Uncle Victor suffered from terrible arthritis – a by-product of WWII, flying B-17s and way too much time in the cold and wet and damp of southeast England. It was time for a rest.

I appreciated being able to tag along. I was too young to hunt; my father had probably been dead for over five years by then and I was happy to be there – even if it was just walking along.

Our rest took the form of squirrel hunting, sitting on the ground next to a tree, remaining quiet and still, and waiting for the little critters to forget about our intrusion and to resume their fall nut-collecting duties. After about forty-five minutes or so, I watched Uncle Victor slowly raise his shotgun (pump 16 gauge, if memory serves), aim at a tree probably forty yards away and wait for the descending squirrel to get a bit closer to the ground. When the squirrel was about four feet off the ground, Uncle Victor fired his round, the squirrel dropped like a rock ... ... and a man simply fell over on his side.

Our world exploded! This older gent had obviously fallen asleep. He had farmer coveralls on, tan in color, a tan overcoat, tan hunting cap. He was simply invisible to us all – until Uncle Victor shot him in his upper-left face. We were totally shocked. He was totally pissed and bleeding like a stuck pig! Words were exchanged – to put it mildly. Luckily, the two men knew each other and the older gent's temper cooled quickly. He was typical of the men and farmers of that era. Now that he knew it was an accident he simply did a ho-hum, I'm bleeding like a stuck pig, I'd better stop it. He pulled a handkerchief from his hip pocket, rejected the call to go to the doctor and just held it over his wounds. Finally, after a clear demand from Uncle Victor, Mike and I were designated to go with him to his car and see him to the doctor.

Slowly we walked … bleed, bleed, bleed … he opened his trunk and slowly wiped down his gun and cased it … bleed, bleed, bleed … he took off his coveralls and folded them before he stowed them away … bleed, bleed, bleed … then, still holding the handkerchief over his wound, he drove to the doctors, where we met up with my Uncle Victor.

Luckily, no real damage was done. His eye was OK, the shallow pellets were removed and the deeper ones were simply left in place. I would see that man on and off for the next half-dozen years or so (until I left home for the military), and up until the last time I saw him, I could see three very clear and distinct black dots on his left forehead – the remaining pellets from our hunting accident.

That story is nearly fifty years old – far older than I care to admit. Yet, it is so vivid – the surprise of the man falling over – even today there is a bit of a catch in my heart. It's a good reminder to:

Always be sure of your target and what's beyond it.

Eye Protection

From the movie *A Christmas Story* (1983) …

> Ralphie: No! No! I want an Official Red Ryder
> Carbine-Action Two-Hundred-Shot Range Model Air
> Rifle!
> Mrs. Parker: No, you'll shoot your eye out.
> Narrator Ralphie: Oh my god, I shot my eye out!

Probably one of the most iconic movies for firearm safety, often quoted as the real reason you do not buy children firearms, for they will surely put their eye out!

I say this a bit tongue in cheek and yet – there is truth from a few points of view. Eyes are NOT replaceable; they are incredibly delicate pieces of equipment that are easily damaged.

Our bodies have developed a number of defensive systems to help us protect our eyes. They are located in extremely close proximity to the brain. As a result, signals for movement, closure of our eye lids, dilatation of the iris and flexing of muscles to manipulate the lens can initiate action much, much faster because the distance to travel through the neural-net is so short.

Eyelids have been provided to cover the eye's surface, protecting it from abrasion and providing some level of protection against penetration.

A cleansing system is built in to constantly clean the eye's surface and to wash away particles that may damage and scar the surface.

The eye's defensive systems have been provided a parallel connection to our body's autonomic nerve system, allowing the eyes to blink and the eyelid to close as soon as it detects a threat. No conscious thought is required to do this. And yet, we can manually control these same functions as well.

All said, the body has done much to protect one of our primary senses – sight. Yet, in the environment in which a shooter finds himself – be it on the range or engaging a threat – the possibility of damage to the eye by foreign bodies abound.

On the range, shrapnel from shattered bullets, components ejected from an exploding firearm, un-burnt powder, hot gases around revolver cylinders or something as simple as an ejected case can do real, severe and permanent damage to your eyes. You can, indeed, shoot your eye out!

In a high threat environment – combat for example – damage from everything as small as a pebble to a shard of an exploding RPG can take a combatant out of the fight for a long time. Even something as simple as a handful of sand thrown in your eye can temporarily blind – something that can easily prove fatal.

Being creative critters, humans have developed supplementary protection for this valuable sense. Today they are Shooting Glasses, Safety Glasses, Protective Lenses – strengthened, typically polycarbonate lenses that are worn in front of our eyes. Our natural defenses are left in place, covered by an additional, transparent layer to help insure our eyes are not penetrated by some type of projectile.

<u>PROTECTIVE SHOOTING GLASSES</u>

Standards, standards, standards . . .

When you purchase a set of shooting glasses to protect your eyes, it's good to know just what kind of protection you are spending money on. Two primary standards have evolved that describe exactly the level of protection you are purchasing. They are defined by **ANSI Z87.1-2003** and **EN 166 (F)**.

The ANSI Standard is a US standard which states that lenses will be divided into two protection levels: Basic Impact and High Impact, as dictated by test criteria. Basic Impact lenses must pass the drop ball test, a 1 diameter steel ball is dropped on the lens from 50 inches.

The EN-166 (F), while mirroring the same Basic Impact requirement, adds a specific test for high velocity impact by requiring the lenses to defend your eyes from a 6mm steel ball weighing 0.86g travelling at least 45 m/s at the time of impact.

These specifications, and manufacturing tests, are what define the word "protection" when it applies to the protection you are purchasing when you pick up a pair of shooting glasses.

The following are a couple of links that can give you a more detailed description of these specifications; they are well worth your time to read through.

http://www.safetyglassesusa.com/ansiz8712003.html
http://www.safetyspecs.co.uk/BS%20EN%20166.htm
http://www.6mmbr.com/eyeprotection.html

My personal choice for eyewear is the **5.11 Raid Eyewear**. Their biggest advantage is three different lens inserts – clear, amber and smoke – that cover the full range of shooting conditions.

So, the next time you are at the range, make sure your eyes are on and that they meet the minimum specifications to protect one of your most important senses … your sight.

The alternative?

You'll put your eye out!

Ear Protection

We experience our world through our five senses – touch, taste, smell, sight and hearing. They allow our bodies to orient themselves, to protect themselves and to provide a defined connection to the world and the people around us. Without them,we are but a bag of meat. With them … I'm Bill.

The loss of any one our senses diminishes our level of integration. A blind person loses the ability to identify people, places or things by sight, so they will switch to identification by sound or smell or touch.

An individual who has lost the sense of touch – perhaps through stroke or accident – relies much more heavily on sight to determine their physical location and orientation.

A loss of smell affects our ability to taste as well – creating a bland and grey world as we take nourishment while losing the enjoyment of varied tastes.

Finally – our sense of sound allows us to identify friend or foe, enjoy the melody of our favorite song or the voice of the one we love.

As shooters, we place two of our senses in harm's way every time we visit the shooting range: our sight and our hearing.

We've discussed the protection of our sight earlier. A malfunctioning weapon, an unfortunate ricochet, an errant casing ejected from our weapon can easily damage our sight. Eye protection is simply a must EVERY TIME YOU STEP ON THE RANGE!

So let's chat about our hearing. A quick review of just how we hear might be useful.

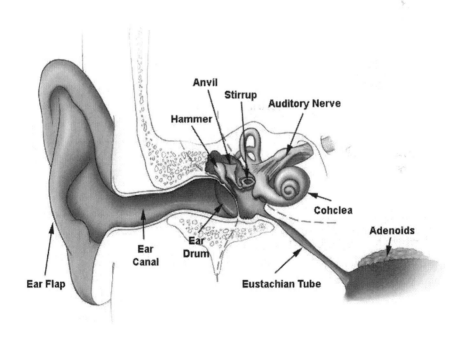

THE HUMAN EAR

The Ear Flap is that combination of skin and cartilage we typically call our ear. Yet, it is but a small part of the overall sensor. Its primary purpose is to gather sound waves and funnel them down the Ear Canal.

The Ear Canal is a channel to the primary hearing sensor components – the Ear Drum, the Hammer, the Anvil and the Stirrup. These are very fragile components, and during the development of our bodies, they migrated deep into our skull – protected by skin and fat and muscle and bone. The combination of the Ear Flap and Ear Canal insures that the gathered sounds find their way to these sensors.

As the sound waves travel down the Ear Canal they encounter the Ear Drum, creating vibrations in this thin, taut membrane of skin. This is one component that can become damaged over time by repeated exposure to high levels of sound, by repeated infection or by rapid changes in pressure.

Attached to the opposite side of the **Ear Drum** is the **Hammer**. It transfers the physical vibration of the **Ear Drum** to the **Anvil,** which then transfers it to the **Stirrup**. Finally, the **Stirrup** is attached to the **Cochlea**. This is a fluid-filled sensor with an attached nerve bundle – the **Auditory Nerve**. As the vibrations of the **Ear Drum** are transferred through the **Stirrup,** the fluid that fills the **Cochlea** receives these vibrations. They are detected by the **Auditory Nerve** and transferred to the brain for interpretation and final conversion to the sounds that we hear. The **Cochlea** performs one additional function for us: it provides us with balance. There are small hairs – **Cilia** – that line the inside of the **Cochlea**. As we move, the fluid within the **Cochlea** also moves, inducing motion of the **Cilia**. This movement is also captured by the **Auditory Nerve** and is transferred to the brain for interpretation of which way is up.

You'll note that the components inside the **Ear Drum** are a sealed system. This means that the pressure from one side of the **Ear Drum** to the other can encounter significant differences. Think how your ears pop as you rise in an aircraft. The differential pressure between the outside and the inside is increasing. Yawning or swallowing or chewing gum act to equalize this pressure. What really happens is that your **Eustachian Tube** is used to equalize this pressure through your open mouth. This is a protection your body provides to insure that your **Ear Drum** doesn't rupture during a rapid change in pressure.

So now that we have reviewed how we hear – how do we lose this ability?

Well – illness, disease and age are common causes of hearing loss. However, as shooters we are at additional risk of hearing loss through repeated exposure to high levels of noise. For comparison – let's look as some typical noises and their levels – typically measured in a unit-of-measure called the decibel (dB).

Painful Noise:
150 dB = Rock Concerts at Peak
140 dB = *Firearms,* Air-Raid Siren, Jet Engine
130 dB = Jackhammer
120 dB = Jet Plane Take-off, Car Stereo, Band Practice

Extremely loud:
110 dB = Machinery, Model Airplanes
100 dB = Snowmobile, Chain saw, Pneumatic Drill
90 dB = Lawnmower, Shop Tools, Truck Traffic, Subway
Very loud:
80 dB = Alarm Clock, Busy Street
70 dB = Vacuum Cleaner
60 dB = Conversation, Dishwasher
Moderate:
50 dB = Moderate Rainfall
40 dB = Quiet Room
Faint:
30 dB = Whisper, Quiet Library

As you can see, most of the average sound levels around us rest in the 50-60 dB levels. Short duration elevations – while possibly painful – will have little long-term effect on our ability to hear. However, frequent or prolonged levels above 70 dB provide a prime opportunity for hearing loss. Those of us who make frequent trips to the range run a real risk of severe and permanent hearing loss. Hence the frequent cry heard on shooting ranges … EARS!

Hearing protection will typically consist of three types:

Simple **Foam Plugs**. These are pushed past the **Ear Flap** and into the **Ear Canal**. Their simple purpose is to absorb some of the high-amplitude sound waves and attenuate their level before they reach the **Ear Drum** and damage it. These are cheap, usually okay for a single use but should not be considered as a long-term solution.

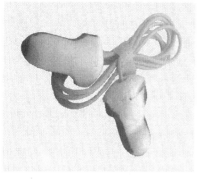

FOAM PLUGS   EAR MUFFS

Ear Muffs surround the **Ear Flap**. They are filled with sound-dampening foam and act to attenuate the sound before it reaches the **Ear Flap**. Variations on this type of hearing protection will provide you with the best long-term solution for hearing protection on the shooting range. And, for very large caliber weapons, a combination of a simple **Foam Plug AND Ear Muffs** will go a long way to insure you will be hearing just fine well into the future.

AMPLIFIED EAR MUFFS

Amplified Ear Muffs are the best of both worlds. They contain an electronic system that uses external microphones to pick up the conversations of those around you and yet, at the first indication of a gunshot, they electronically turn off the microphones and provide you a full level of protection for your hearing. I find their only downfall is that I consistently forget to turn off the amplifiers and drain the batteries. Still, they are great for the range when you want to carry on a conversation without having to remove your ear protection to hear the other person.

There's a reason everyone hears "EARS!" on the range – take care of your hearing. Once it's gone … it's gone!

Choosing a range

How does a new shooter go about finding a place to shoot? In my younger days, I could simply go into my back yard or a near-by wood lot and blast away. For most people those days are long since gone. So how do you do it?

Well, there is undoubtedly a local shooting community, but it might just take a little digging to find it. One great resource is your local police officers. Many shoot competitively to sharpen their work-day shooting skills, and they do this at a local range. Gun stores, local clubs like the Izaac Walton League or other conservation groups can point you in the right direction as well. Your shooting instructor (assuming you have taken class recently) will certainly have a location set aside for his class that many times will offer memberships as well.

One resource I am typically leery of is un-managed public shooting ranges. We have a couple of these in my area, and they can be a disquieting experience. Not everyone obeys the four rules of gun safety. Not everyone goes to the range sober. Not everyone is trustworthy. While I have made very limited use of a range near one of my course locations, I don't make a habit of it.

What can you expect from a local shooting club? In my experience there are lots of friendly people there, all interested in the same sport you are. These folks are a great resource. Most will be willing to lend a hand if you need it, answer questions if you have them and – in many cases – give you the opportunity to try their weapons if you have a mind to.

Managed ranges will typically have a clear set of range rules that you will be expected to know. Many times these will be gone over with you either individually or as a group at the beginning of the shooting season by the range's RSO (Range Safety Officer). Many of these types of ranges are secured, requiring either a pin number, lock combination or swipe card to gain entry. These are all good things. It clearly shows the range takes its responsibilities seriously and it provides you a level of comfort that shooters are all starting out with the same clear view of the range's rules and expectations.

Many managed ranges will have specific limitations set within their range rules. These may include: No draw from a holster, limits on the caliber of ammunition, limits on the number or rounds per second, the number of times a friend may be admitted as a guest, the type of ammunition used … to name just a few possibilities. Please, take the time to meet with their RSO for a complete range safety briefing; it may save some hard feelings down the road. And, make sure that the type of training you want, and the skill set you want to practice are available and permitted at the range. If they are not, keep looking!

Prices will vary, and dues are usually a two-tiered structure, first for club membership and then with an additional fee being required as a range fee. Shooting ranges require constant attention, supervision and observation, not to mention additional costs for target stands, steel targets, berm maintenance – all of which make the shooting sports a bit more expensive. I would expect most club fees would be from $50 to $150 per year with an additional $20+ for a range fee. It is also not unusual for additional fees to be required if you decide to enter different shooting competitions (on a per competition basis) at the range as well.

The biggest plus for you in joining a recognized shooting club in your area is simply your access to other shooters. I learn each and every time I shoot with a new partner. And they learn from me as well. Clubs bring us all together. Find a club, join and enjoy; a new competitive season is just around the corner!

Range day – what to bring

You need to schedule range days, as often as possible, every month – including winter. Then, you need to keep the schedule – rain, shine, sunny, cloudy, calm, windy, hot, cold, dry, wet, rain, snow, ice. The guy/gal who picks you as a target, who intends to rob you, beat you, kill you will not wait for a gorgeous summer day, (ok, he/she might), so your range time needs to cover all the bases. Once scheduled, what do you bring? I'm going to split this up into three sections – **Clothing,** your **Range Bag** and **Miscellaneous** stuff.

Clothing:

Dress for the weather – although I routinely recommend long pants that are a loose fit rather than shorts. If it's cold – a solid layering system that allows you to shed some clothing if your range work heats you up. But, in general, here's the list:

- Hat (I prefer a baseball cap so the bill covers my face over my shooting glasses.)
- Comfortable shirt with a high neck or collar. (This is especially important for women.)
- Comfortable pants
- Sturdy shoes and hiking socks (Once had a lady show up in January wearing high-heel boots). No open toed shoes or sandals
- Bandana
- Rain gear – rain pants and coat, not a poncho (you shoot, regardless of whether it's pouring or not)

- You may want knee pads, depending on the drills you intend to run.
- Strong side holster
- Minimum of two magazine holders or speed-loader holders
- Sturdy pistol belt
- Shooting gloves if your drills call for them

Range Bag:
- Your weapon (no, really, double check!)
- Minimum of three magazines or speed loaders – more is better
- Ammunition for your drills (also, really, double check!)
- Hearing protection
- Eye protection
- A small set of tools
- Cleaning kit
- Stapler with extra staples
- First aid kit – primarily for cuts and nicks
- A BOK (Blow Out Kit) for if the unthinkable happens
- Notebook for shooting notes on your drills
- Targets specific to any drills that you may need
- Timer if needed for your drills (Note: there are a number of free apps for that.)

Miscellaneous:
- Sun screen (you burn, sunny or cloudy)
- Chap stick
- Something to eat (jerky, food bars – I usually skip the sandwiches)
- Something to drink (water, soda, juice – more than you think you should bring)
- Sweat towel – a standard hand towel; I always carry an OD towel – shooting, hiking, canoeing or just riding in my Jeep

Finally, develop a plan. Your first trips, I would recommend doing everything from the compressed high-ready. Firm grip on your weapon, your weapon held center chest with the barrel parallel to the ground. I prefer a modified weaver stance – feet shoulder width apart, dominant side foot back about one foot's length from the support side foot. The drills are limited to extension and release of safety (if needed), target acquisition, target engagement with a random number of rounds (1 to 3), engaging the safety (again, if needed) and bringing your weapon back to a compressed high-ready.

Your plan should include a number of different drills (see http://pistol-training.com for some ideas) and also should include snap-caps to simulate weapon malfunctions.

Limit your time to an hour. After an hour people naturally lose their ability to focus and concentrate. Speed is NOT your goal – being smooth and accurate is. Complete each step – extension, safety release, target acquisition, target engagement, engaging the safety, returning to the compressed high-ready – PERFECTLY. Slow down if you are sloppy. Speed up until you get sloppy. You are training muscle memory during these sessions so when the fellow with the gun, knife, ax, machete is getting ready to send you to your Maker, you can change the situation without having to think through the steps. Speed comes with time, as do holster draws. For now, for your first few trips, let's work on these basics first. We'll talk about the rest later.

A look at what's in my bag:

FIRST AID KIT   TOOL KIT

Bill Keller

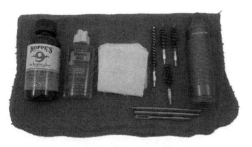

GUN CLEANING KIT

SHOOTING GLASSES

EAR MUFFS

EAR PLUGS

RANGE BAG

STAPLE GUN AND STAPLES

Range Rules and Commands

Rule: a prescribed guide for conduct or action; an accepted procedure, custom, or habit

Command: to direct authoritatively, to exercise a dominating influence over

I conducted an NRA Basic Pistol course recently and was reviewing some range tape. I look for a number of things – am I being attentive, what am I missing, is my manner helpful, are my commands clear and consistent – there's a lot to watch for. In this last class, the majority of the students were new shooters – a couple had never touched a weapon of any kind. One of their greatest fears is the range time, where they are expected to properly and safely pick up a handgun, load it and accurately fire it. They get nervous, a little fearful. During the classroom portion leading up to range time, we simulate the entire process in the classroom and I give each student a chance to dry fire the weapon they will be using. And I cover the **Range Rules and Commands**. I warn them twenty-one years in the military has left a bit of an edge in my range voice and demeanor. Actually, it's mellowed significantly – yet its presence is still enough to insure that the students do listen and follow my commands.

Just what are these **Range Rules and Commands**? New shooters who have no range time imagine all sorts of things – from the screaming Drill Instructor to the trigger-happy redneck. Let's take a walk through the **Rules and Commands**.

Each range is different in many respects. However, there is a core that is used at the vast majority of shooting ranges throughout the country; that's where I would like to spend my time.

Safety Rules: These are the basics. While there are variants – the NRA basic safety rules are hard to beat.

ALWAYS keep your firearm pointed in a safe direction.
ALWAYS keep your finger off the trigger until you are ready to shoot.
ALWAYS keep your firearm unloaded until you are ready to use it.

A fourth is typically added:
ALWAYS make sure what is in front of – and behind – your target.

Additional rules concerning the condition of your firearms, fields of fire, hours of operation – to mention just a few – will be contained in your range's range brief. Pay attention; it could save your life.

Range Commands: On a shooting range, on a firing line – commands are just that – commands! They are not suggestions, general thoughts, good ideas – they are words that demand a specific course of action. With a single exception, they are issued by the RSO or the Training Officer (TO) in charge of the range. Let's talk about the exception first, and then the individual range commands.

CEASE FIRE! CEASE FIRE! CEASE FIRE! - The Cease Fire command may be given by anyone on the range – ANYONE! Its purpose is to immediately stop all shooting on the range. There may be a person or child wandering around in front of the firing line (this just happened near our community – the eight-year-old child received a .22 Cal round to the head – jury is still out if he will live). There may have been a shooting accident, or a profoundly unsafe act by a shooter on the line, or a medical emergency just behind the line (think heart attack or fainting spell). Something of significance has happened and all shooting needs to stop. The command CEASE FIRE! is said three times in a loud voice. If you as a shooter hear that command, stop firing IMMEDIATELY, put your weapon on safe, and stand at the low ready (weapon pointed down at a 45-degree angle, safety on, finger off the trigger) until someone tells you what to do. Follow all commands given – don't guess or suppose.

Step to the Firing Line - Going to the firing line is at the invitation of the RSO or the Training Officer (TO). (Yes, I know, many ranges do not have either on duty 24/7 – these commands will apply primarily during course work or competition. Yet, following many of these procedures while you are there – on your own – will make for a safer experience.) When you hear this, you will step to the firing line with an unloaded weapon.

Load and Make Ready - Insert your loaded magazine, or close your loaded cylinder, or close the loading gate on your Single Action (SA) revolver, or operate the bolt on your rifle to put a round in the chamber, or operate the slide on your pump to put a round in the chamber. When you complete this command, your weapon is loaded, your safety is on and it is ready to fire.

Ready on the right? Ready on the left? Ready on the firing line? Or **Are the shooters ready?** RSO or the TO are asking you if you are ready to go. If you are NOT (something didn't load right, something feels off) TELL THEM NO, explain to them the issue and have them assist you in clearing it. Do not begin shooting just because everyone else does – make sure you are truly ready to begin the drill.

Your Course of Fire Is . . . I will usually, at this point, remind students what the course of fire is. New shooters can have a million things going through their minds, and it helps to focus and settle them.

Commence Fire - Begin your drill. DO NOT PRESS THE TRIGGER UNTIL THIS COMMAND IS GIVEN!

Stand-By - This command is typically limited to shooting competitions. It is given just prior to the Timer pressing the start button on the shooting timer. You will then hear a delayed beep! (typically within 2-4 seconds) that gives you permission to Commence Fire.

Unload and Show Clear - This command can actually be given any time. If the RSO or TO wants to safe the range, one of the first things they will ask you to do is to unload your weapon. Release the magazine or open the cylinder and eject the cartridges or open the loading gate on your SA revolver and eject the cartridges. For semi-automatic pistols, lock the slide back, hold the weapon in your dominant hand, hold your magazine in your support hand and hold them next to each other so the RSO or TO can clearly see an empty chamber and an empty (or partially loaded) magazine. For a Double Action (DA) revolver, have the cylinder open and all cartridges removed. Hold it so the RSO or TO can clearly see the empty cylinder. For an SA revolver, have the loading gate open, the hammer half-cocked so the cylinder rotates freely and spin it slowly so the RSO or TO can see all chambers are empty.

Thank You! - I may be the only one to use this command. I say it after the Unload and Show Clear when I have physically observed that the shooter's weapon is, indeed, unloaded and clear. It is my acknowledgement to the shooter that the process is complete.

MUZZLE! - This command is usually said in a loud and curt voice. It means you have swept the muzzle of your weapon across a part of another shooter's body. I will give a single warning. The next occurrence earns an immediate ejection from the range and the activity of the day.

The Range (course) is COLD - A cold range or course means that a weapon may be loaded only at the firing line and at the command of the RSO or TO. You may load magazines or load your cylinder, leaving the cylinder or loading gate open, but you may not Load and Make Ready until you are invited to the firing line and given the command. This may be the policy of the entire range (as it is at our range) or simply for the duration of the course you are taking.

The Range (course) is HOT - A hot range or course means that you may keep your weapon topped off and load empty magazines when you have the opportunity. This is typical in the more advanced run and gun course, which is limited to more advanced shooters. Actually, this is real life; when you are carrying your weapon on a daily basis, you are Range HOT. Keep your head in the game during these courses; your life and those of your fellow students depend on you doing everything perfectly.

These are not just words … they are words to be safe by … they are words to live by.

Pay attention …
Keep your head in the game …
Lives depend on it . . . .

Trust NO ONE!

Trusting a fellow shooter can get you hurt – or dead. My personal example:

A very good friend of mine had a .45 Cal 1911 worked on quite some time back. He was very happy with the job and was anxious to show me. It was a defensive weapon that he kept on an upper bookshelf in his den. He reached for it, dropped the magazine and went to hand it to me. I asked him to check the chamber. "Don't worry; there isn't a round in the chamber. " I acknowledged he was probably right, I just asked him to humor me. And he did – imagine his surprise as a cartridge was ejected as he racked the slide. Was I angry? Nope. While it's fully his responsibility to know the state of his weapon and to only hand it to me when he is sure it is safe, (and he was sure), it is MY RESPONSIBILITY to know that each and every weapon handed to me is safe – PERIOD. Do not depend on someone else to save you, to protect you or to prevent you from being harmed – it is YOUR JOB to do that and no one else's.

In my classes, I display over a dozen firearms. Double and single action revolvers, .22 Cal, 9mm and .45 Cal semi-automatic pistols and even a 6mm airsoft pistol. The images below show you how I present them to the students. The action is open, the cylinder open, the loading gate open and all magazines out. They stay this way throughout the entire course, and any time a firearm is passed from me to a student or from one student to another, the chamber and the magazine are double checked before the exchange happens. This should be done in all firearms classes – period. If it's not – remember your safety is YOUR RESPONSIBILITY. Don't surrender your safety to anyone – check each and every firearm to make sure the magazine is out, the slide is locked back, the chamber is empty, the cylinder is open or the loading gate is open.

Remember, help is not coming, you are not going to be saved, you are responsible for your own survival and safety – period – YOU.

RUGER 22/45 MK III

DOUBLE ACTION REVOLVER

SINGLE ACTION REVOLVER

GLOCK

SPRINGFIELD ARMORY 1911

RUGER LC9

CHAPTER 2 – WHAT MAKES IT GO BLAM?

AS YOU STAND AT THE FIRING LINE, GRIP YOUR weapon and press the trigger – you are waiting for a single event to happen ... BLAM!

Why does it do that? There is a thousand years' plus worth of history behind the reason. It's a history worth knowing – from the development of gunpowder, through the evolution of today's cartridge to the general components of a firearm.

All controlled by you – the shooter.

Let's take a walk through history and find out just what makes it go BLAM!

Once you hear that magic sound, a projectile is on its way! For the handgun shooter, this projectile, this bullet, takes many different shapes. So let's chat a bit about bullets, their composition and their different shapes. Then let's pick some specific bullets for specific tasks.

Part 1

You've loaded your firearm, taken your stance, have a firm grip, a solid site alignment, you have a good sight picture ... you press the trigger ... BLAM! Why does it do that?

What Makes It Go BLAM?

While many things can propel a projectile that has enough velocity and mass to penetrate a human (or animal) and inflict a killing wound, for the purpose of this discussion, let's confine ourselves to handguns, long guns and shotguns.

The reason a firearm goes BLAM! Is this:

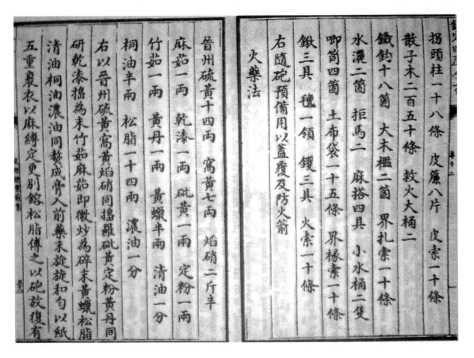

CHINESE RECIPE FOR GUN POWDER

The development date varies, but by as early as the 7th century, China had developed the above formula for a mixture of Potassium Nitrate (or Saltpeter), Charcoal and Sulfur into a compound that is today known generically as **Gunpowder**. Beginning with a basic formula of 76% Potassium Nitrate, 14% Charcoal and 10% Sulfur, they developed at least six different formulas for use in everything from hand cannons to rocket-propelled arrows:

CHINESE HAND CANNON

CHINESE ROCKET-PROPELLED ARROWS

The basic chemical reaction is that the sulfur is ignited; this begins a chemical reaction with the Potassium Nitrate that releases oxygen to sustain the reaction and nitrogen. This increases the temperature enough to ignite the charcoal – which then releases larger quantities of carbon dioxide and monoxide. This reaction continues until the accelerant (the potassium nitrate, since it accelerates the chemical reaction) and the fuel (the charcoal and sulfur) are consumed. The resultant gases – a mixture of carbon dioxide, carbon monoxide, nitrogen and a tad of sulfur dioxide) – are the true propellants that expel the bullet down the barrel of the hand cannon, hand gun, long gun, shotgun or shoot the rocket into the air.

28

Of course, to use this chemical reaction most efficiently, the combustion of these materials must be confined and the discharge of the gases must be aimed – hence the development of a long cylinder, the barrel, strong enough to hold the hot gases – yet with a hole to both direct the gases and to control the direction of the projectile.

Early weapons depended on fuses that were embedded with **Gunpowder**. Once lit, they delivered fire through a small port in the barrel that ignited the weapon's charge, which then fired, sending gas and projectile down the barrel. This controlled explosion of **Gunpowder** is, indeed, the BLAM that we all hear on the firing line or in the field when we gently press the trigger to the rear until the hammer strikes the firing pin in a modern day weapon.

Early weapons evolved into the next most prevalent firearm – the **Flintlock**.

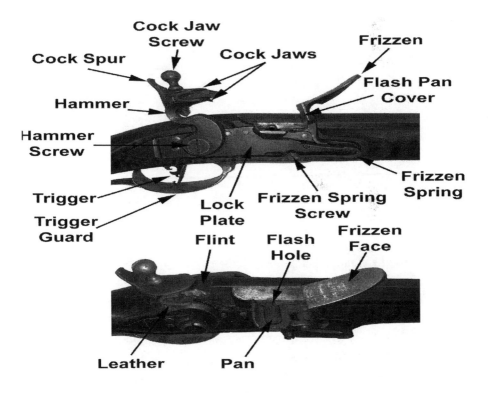

FLINTLOCK MUZZLELOADER COMPONENTS

One of the earliest and most reliable ways to build a fire was with flint and steel. A piece of flint is struck with a piece of steel and the collision is enough to generate an energized particle of steel we call a spark. The temperature of this spark is high enough to ignite **Gunpowder**.

One of the earliest weapons to take advantage of this was the **Flintlock** rifle or pistol.

FLINTLOCK MUZZLELOADER PROJECTILES

Basically the weapon is upended. A measured **Powder Charge** is poured into the end of the barrel. A projectile – usually a **Ball**, surrounded by a **Wad** – is fit down the barrel and rammed to the bottom of the barrel. A small amount of **Gunpowder** is poured into the **Pan**. A piece of flint is locked into the hammer and, when the trigger is pressed, the hammer strikes its flint against the **Frizzen**, (a steel plate), generating a spark. This spark ignites the powder in the **Pan**; its fire then travels through a flash hole in the side of the barrel, ignites the **Powder Charge** within the barrel and … BLAM!

In the interest of reliability – the **Powder** in the **Pan** could easily become damp and not ignite; the flint and steel were eventually replaced by **Primers**.

The **Primer** is essentially what you see today in the rear of a center fire cartridge. The material on the inside of the **Primer** ignites when it is struck sharply. Again, the fire generated by striking the **Primer** travels through the flash hole in the barrel and ignites the charge at the bottom of the barrel and ... BLAM!

3 PRIMERS AND NIPPLE

The focus changed from the **Flintlock** aspect of firing the weapon to the **Muzzle Loading** aspect of the weapon. So, even though the basics of loading the weapon did not change from a **Flintlock Rifle** (or pistol) to a **Muzzle Loading Rifle** (or pistol), from this point on they were called by the loading process – **Muzzle Loaders**.

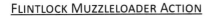

As these weapons became the weapon of choice in armed conflict, the need to load them quicker became apparent. The development of the **Cartridge** began.

Early efforts were to simply combine the **Powder Charge** and the **Bullet** and/or shot into a single paper-wrapped **Cartridge**.

FLINTLOCK MUZZLELOADER ACTION

31

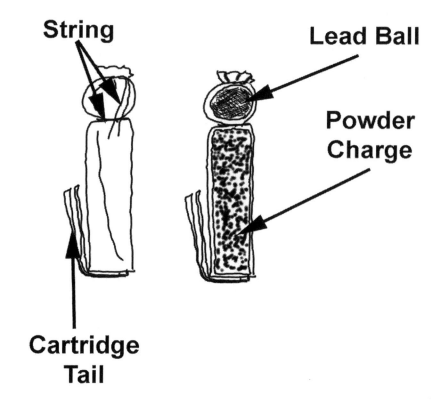

FLINTLOCK MUZZLELOADER PAPER CARTRIDGE

To load the weapon, the bottom is torn off; the **Powder Charge** is poured down the barrel and the paper wrapping the **Bullet** acts as the **Wad** to allow the **Bullet** and/or shot to be tamped down the barrel. This process eliminated the need to measure **Powder**, prepare a **Wad**, tamp the **Bullet** and prime the weapon. Simply tearing, tamping, priming (inserting a new **Primer Cap**) and BLAM, greatly increased the rate of fire of the single soldier.

The final step was the development of the modern day **Cartridge** – essentially unchanged for over 150 years.

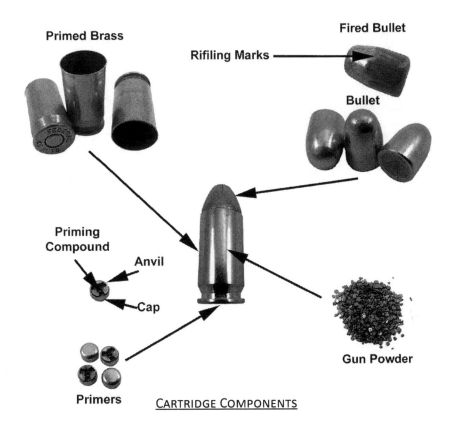

CARTRIDGE COMPONENTS

The **Case** (1) is the chassis that holds all the components together. Today it is typically made of brass (you can reload these), steel (one shot only) or aluminum (again, one shot only). Pressed into the center of the rear of the **Casing** (think center fire) is the (2) **Primer**. The **Primer Mix** ignites when struck sharply by the **Firing Pin**. In the center of the **Anvil** is a flash hole . The **Anvil** insures a small amount of **Gunpowder** is very close to the **Primer Mix**. The **Primer** is struck, the **Primer Mix** ignites, the flame travels through the flash hole, it ignites the **Gunpowder** (3), and the gas expands and propels the **Bullet** (4) down the **Barrel**, out the **Muzzle** – BLAM!

This final development, the self-contained **Cartridge**, again significantly increased the rate of fire of the soldier on the battle field. Next were the developments in the actions that allowed for a mechanical increase in the rate at which an expended **Cartridge** could be replaced with a **Cartridge** that was ready to fire. But … that's for another segment.

So, to recap, why does our weapon go BLAM?

Gunpowder - confined, rapidly generated gas - gas expelled down a **Barrel** behind a **Bullet** - **Bullet** exits the **Barrel** at the **Muzzle** - BLAM!

And there ya go – BLAM!

Part 2: the Barrel

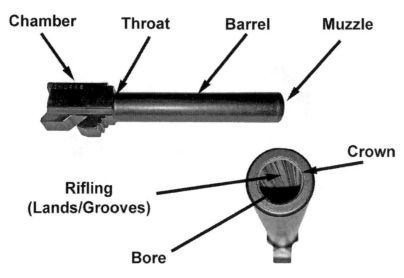

In **Part 1** we discussed, in depth, the cartridge and its evolution through the centuries. It is the component that holds the projectile – the bullet or shot. It is the first item required for a weapon to go BLAM! However, simply having a cartridge go "BLAM!" is of little use to us. We need the ability to control the direction of the bullet that is ejected from the casing when the powder ignites. The part of a firearm that provides this control is the **Barrel**.

What purpose does a **Barrel** serve? Actually, it serves four distinct functions:

1. It receives the cartridge.

2. It contains the explosion of the cartridge and focuses the resulting pressure.

3. It aims the projectile.

4. It increases the accuracy of the projectile.

It receives the cartridge

The cartridge exits the magazine and is driven forward into the chamber by the bolt. The bullet extends from the chamber into the throat – the very beginning of the bore - the hole that extends through the center of the **Barrel**. The bore is microscopically narrower than the bullet. It has a number of grooves machined down it that are given a slight twist – this is called **Rifling**. This results in part of the bore being higher (**Lands**) than the grooves that are machined out (**Grooves**). This allows the bore to slightly grip the bullet as it exits, spinning it and increasing its overall accuracy. The end of the **Barrel** has a slight inward crown machined into it that allows an even distribution of the gasses as they exit the region at the end of the barrel – the **Muzzle**.

There are exceptions to everything, including the **Rifling** of rifle barrels. There are smooth bore rifles – primarily replicas of early types of firearms or some very advanced military arms that fire guided projectiles. And, the standard shotgun has a smooth bore as well. Shotguns used to fire slugs and will either utilize a special rifled slug or will have interchangeable barrels so a rifled barrel can be swapped in.

It contains the explosion of the cartridge and focuses the resulting pressure

The explosive power of a cartridge – be it pistol, rifle, shotgun or cannon – is massive. The primary characteristics of the cartridge that determine its chamber pressure are the powder composition (which determines its burn rate and overall energy content) and the quantity of powder. Chamber fit also comes into play, since the bullet MUST be able to escape the **Barrel**. An oversized bullet jammed into a normal sized chamber will guarantee an overpressure situation and the destruction of the **Barrel**. This can also be accomplished by an improper powder charge as well. The results, should the pressure NOT be contained, would look something like this:

`CATASTROPHIC BARREL FAILURE

When everything works properly – the cartridge is properly seated, the firing pin or striker strikes the center of the primer, the primer ignites the powder, the gases from the powder rapidly expand, the explosion is contained and focused, the bullet exits the case, the bore – with its **Rifling** – grabs the bullet, spins it and it exits the **Barrel** at the **Muzzle** at proper velocity in the direction the **Barrel** is aimed. The **Barrel** is an integral component of harnessing the energy of the BLAM!

It aims the projectile

The centerline of the bore is machined to be perfectly parallel with the **Barrel**. An aiming device is attached to the **Barrel** to assist the shooter to direct his shot. Front and rear iron sights can be used to align the **Barrel** with the intended target. A telescopic sight is used for long-distance shots. Holographic sights are used for close quarter battle and rapid acquisition shooting. But all share a common goal – to properly align the **Barrel** with the target to insure that when the trigger is pressed and the cartridge goes BLAM, the bullet that exits the **Muzzle** hits the intended target – be it a piece of paper or an imminent threat.

It increases the accuracy of the projectile

As described earlier, the bore is machined in such a way as to create **Lands** and **Grooves** - **Rifling**. The **Rifling** grabs the bullet as it travels down the **Barrel**, inducing a spin in the bullet. The concept is the same as throwing a football that spins in a spiral as it travels towards a receiver, or the fletching on the rear of an arrow that spins the arrow as it travels towards its target.

A spinning projectile has increased gyroscopic stability, allowing it to travel longer distances much more accurately.

When everything is combined, the cartridge is loaded, the explosion is contained, and the bullet exits the **Barrel** with a spin induced by the **Rifling**. And you, as the shooter, hear that lovely sound that results from this process …

BLAM!

TYPICAL PROJECTILE

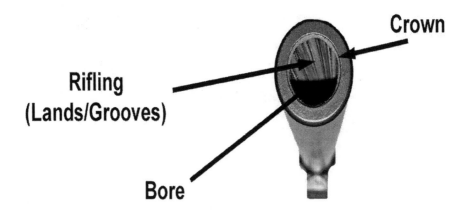

Crown

Rifling
(Lands/Grooves)

Bore

BARREL WITH RIFLING

Part 3 - The Action Is Where The Action Is

In **Part 1,** we discussed the development of gunpowder, different types of early firearms and finally how all that led to the development of the modern day cartridge.

Next, in **Part 2,** we discussed the characteristics of the **Barrel** – the component that contains and focuses the energy of the cartridge and then increases the accuracy of the projectile after the cartridge is fired.

In this section, I want to discuss **Part 3**, the **Action**. As I say in the title, the **Action** is "Where The Action is." What you see in the photo are the major components of the **Action** of my Winchester .45 Cal Long Colt saddle gun. I want to discuss the **Action** in generalities first, and then we'll poke our noses into the details a bit more.

The **Action** knits five major elements together into a usable weapon. Those components are the **Stock**; the **Barrel**; the **Magazine**; the **Mechanical Components** needed to: eject a spent cartridge, insert a new cartridge in the chamber, cock the hammer, release the hammer to strike the firing pin; firing the cartridge; and, finally, **you, the Shooter**. These elements are present in the **Action** regardless of the weapon system. Here I am showing a lever-action rifle. Yet you can find matching or equivalent components in a single-action revolver, double-action revolver, semi-automatic pistol, 105 howitzer – they are all there.

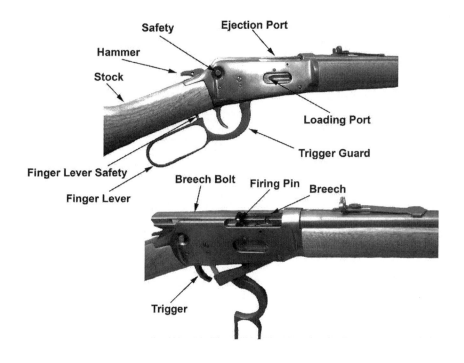

WINCHESTER 94 ACTION

In the modern day carbine, the metal housing that holds these major components together is called the **Receiver**. Yet, its purpose is the same – to join stock, barrel, magazine, mechanical components and human together into an effective and useful weapon.

Let's talk about common components of the **Action**:

The **Lever** is the mechanical component used to eject expended casings from the weapon and push a new round into the chamber.

The **Breech** is the area of the weapon where an expended cartridge begins its exit from the weapon and a new cartridge is placed before it is rammed into the chamber.

The **Breech Bolt** acts as the ejection tool to remove a spent casing, and the ram to insert a new cartridge into the chamber. It contains the **Firing Pin**, which will fire the cartridge when the **Trigger** is pressed, and it is part of the containment system to contain the energy of the cartridge and help force its gasses down the **Barrel** and out the **Muzzle**.

The **Finger Lever** is the component that harnesses the work done by the shooter's hand and allows him to expel an expended cartridge and ram a new cartridge into the chamber.

The **Trigger** is the component that releases the **Firing Pin**.

The **Trigger Guard** is provided to protect the shooter from an unintended discharge due to clothing, brush or other items the **Trigger** may bump against.

This particular weapon has dual safeties – one just rear of the **Breech Bolt** and one between the **Finger Lever** and the **Stock**. The lever must be gripped and the safety released for the weapon to fire.

The **Stock** attaches to the rear of the **Receiver** and the **Barrel**, with a **Tubular Magazine**, (for this particular weapon), attaches to the front of the **Receiver**.

Thus, with **Stock**, **Barrel**, **Magazine**, internal components to eject, insert and fire cartridges, and a shooter to firmly grasp the weapon and aim, shoot and operate it – the weapon system is complete.

Now, picture in your mind's eye the weapons we have detailed and discussed earlier. It's not difficult to see how either the exact same component (think **Trigger**), or very similar components (think **Breech Bolt**) are present in all of them.

With the addition of the **Action** to a weapon, all elements are there … finely tuned … finely crafted … specifically made for each other … so when the time is right … it goes … BLAM!

Yet, there is a final component absent … and that will be the topic of our next – and final – installment of …

What Makes It Go … BLAM!

Part 4: This – and ONLY This – Makes it go BLAM!

In **Part 1,** we covered the chemistry of the BLAM.

In **Part 2,** we covered containment and direction of the energy produced by the chemistry of the BLAM.

In **Part 3,** we covered the mechanics of releasing the chemistry of the BLAM.

In our final segment, we get to the heart of the matter – the one true element that marries all the components listed above into the single, solitary explosion of sound – the BLAM!

You! Your finger!

This - and ONLY this
Makes it go BLAMMMM!!!!

There is one – and ONLY one – thing responsible for the discharge of a weapon – you. We've all heard the excuses:

- I didn't know it was loaded.
- I couldn't fit it in my holster – so I jammed it!
- I couldn't get it out of my holster – so I pulled really hard.
- It was dark – I didn't know who it was – so I shot them.
- I trusted him when he said it was empty.
- We were just fooling around.

. . . . and the thousands more . . . .

And yet, in all the death, pain and mayhem that are represented by these excuses, at the end of the day the shooter – you – are the only thing that makes your weapon go BLAM.

I've written this book for my students and for new shooters. Old heads with years of miles on them in the use and handling of weapons have seen the results of a trigger press, have zipped friends into bags to begin the journey back home, have seen shooters on the range who are alive simply by God's good humor and know the truth of the image. They've seen the ease with which a bullet can destroy. They know it is the last 1/3 of the last joint of their trigger finger that is responsible for the weapon's firing. And nothing else.

However, new shooters with few miles are still coming to grips with the basics of our craft. In their heads they know the truth of the image – in their physical training, their muscle memory, in their personal experience – they are not there yet. If we, as a shooting community, do nothing other than teach them the four basic rules of gun safety and instill in them the sense of responsibility that comes with gun ownership and with carrying a weapon for personal protection, we will have done our job.

The rest is up to the individual shooter … because … at the end of the day … it is YOU, and ONLY YOU … who make it go … BLAM!

Bullets

Projectile: *a body projected by external force and continuing in motion by its own inertia; especially: a missile for a weapon (as a firearm)*

Bullet: *a round or elongated missile (as of lead) to be fired from a firearm; broadly*

Hardness: *resistance of metal to indentation under a static load or to scratching*

Brinell hardness test: *use of a 10mm diameter hardened steel or carbide ball to determine the hardness of a metal*
Frangible: *readily or easily broken*

As with any topic, the more you drill down, the more complicated it becomes. Still, there is a basic level of information a person actually needs to understand a specific topic.

When you start talking about **Bullets**, especially in today's remarkably uninformed world, it's easy for things to go off the rails pretty quickly. I want to take some time to flesh out the basics of **Bullets**, because when you begin the discussion of ammunition selection, use of your weapon and how that affects your **Bullet** selection – I want you to understand the basics.

While the subject matter of **Bullets** is vast, I want to focus on some specific areas:

What is a bullet? Sounds simple, but folks easily mix terms like **Cartridge** and **Bullet**.

What is its composition? Heck – it's lead, right? Not so fast there, Skippy.

Penetration. You are responsible for every round you fire – and everything it penetrates. **Bullet** selection matters.

Basic Shapes. Bullets fit into three basic categories – **Round Nose, Hollow Point** and **Wad Cutter**. There are variations on each theme, but these are the starting point.

Bullet Selection. On the range or on the street – which **Bullet** is best?

What is a **Bullet**?

A **Bullet** is a projectile. It enables the shooter to deliver force at a distance. Before gunpowder and the bow, force was delivered up close and personal through the use of a stone, club, knife, spear, axe, sword. Of course, spears could be thrown, allowing the thrower some separation and a higher level of safety, but still – it was personal.

Humans, looking for an advantage over prey or foe, have continually looked for an advantage in weapons. One interesting innovation was the Atlatl.

Atlatl

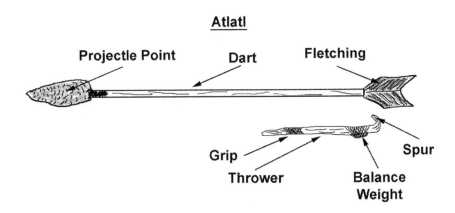

A hand-held throwing tool that effectively lengthened the thrower's arm, increasing the moment of force and allowing the thrower to increase both his distance and killing force. Not sure why, but these are just cool to me!

A sling follows the same idea but uses smooth, rounded stones or – in later years – hand cast lead projectiles as the projectile. They, too, allowed the delivery of a killing force at a greater distance.

We progressed to the bow – a weapon used to this day with great effect and at a great distance.

Enter … **Gunpowder**.

Which led to hand cannons.

Which led to hand guns … and the weapons we are all familiar with today.

Through the use of a handgun, loaded with a **Cartridge** that actually contains the **Bullet** – a modern day shooter can deliver this projectile over great distance with devastating results.

So, at its core, throughout a fairly distinct development history, a **Bullet** is simply a projectile used to deliver force at a distance.

What is a Bullet's composition?

Lead, of course, is the answer that comes so easily. When I think of **Bullets** and bullet casting I think of the scene from The Patriot that has Benjamin Martin hand casting a round-ball from the small lead toy soldiers that were his dead son's toy. And, yes, the vast majority of **Bullets** on the market today are made, substantially, of lead. However, **Bullets** are almost never simply soft lead, but rather an alloy of three different metals – lead, tin and antimony. While the recipe is infinitely variable – in general the mix ratio is around 93% lead, 4% antimony and 3% tin. The use of an alloy affects the hardness of the **Bullet**.

Bullet hardness can be measured by a number of different units of

43

measure. **Bullet** manufacturers typically use the Brinell Scale. This is determined by the direct measurement of a dimple caused in the alloy when a 10mm diameter sphere made of either hardened steel or carbide is pressed into the alloy with a known force (dependent on the alloy) for a defined period of time. The dimple is then measured under a microscope, fed into a standard formula and the result is the hardness of the alloy. Pure lead has a BH of around 5. It is easily scratched with a thumb nail. Cast **Bullets** with the alloy list above run a BH around 15-30, depending on your after-casting Oven/Quench process. The Brinell hardness of hardened copper, probably the most common plating for **Bullets**, is 12. Why is this number important?

Simply put, the softer the **Bullet**, the more metal is scraped off as the **Bullet** travels down the barrel. This is known as leading. As the lands and grooves grasp the **Bullet** to impart their spin, they can peel off lead, the grooves can become clogged and your accuracy will become diminished. This is solved by a good cleaning with a lead solvent, but repeated leading over a prolonged period of time will damage a barrel.

Harder **Bullets** mean less (or no) leading. So your **Bullet composition** – especially if you move to casting your own **Bullets** – is important.

Frangible Bullets: **Bullets** may also be made of frangible material – designed to shatter/break apart upon impact. These **Bullets** are designed specifically to limit penetration. As soon as they meet true resistance, they break apart. Probably the most common use of this style of **Bullet** is in shoot houses where the shooter needs to experience the sounds, smells and feel of a standard round being discharged – but where the danger due to wall penetration or ricochet needs to be reduced.

Solid Coppers: In some areas, concerns of lead pollution are so high – shooters are required to shoot solids only – typically solid copper **Bullets**. You also find trends to reduce lead in shotgun shells, with some states/hunting areas requiring steel shot rather than lead. Are these real dangers? Honestly, I do not think so, but many are of the opposite opinion. Regardless, copper **Bullets** and steel shot are here to stay.

Exotic Bullets: **Bullets** reflect the task at hand – whether target shooting, putting down an animal, killing a terrorist or stopping an armored vehicle. For the latter task, lead or copper **Bullets** would have little effect. However, a 30mm **Bullet** from a GAU-8 Avenger made of depleted uranium would pass through the armor like a hot knife through soft butter. With a weight of .66 pounds, a Brinell Number of 750 and a velocity of approximately 3,000 fps – there is little in the way of armor that can withstand such a **Bullet**.

There are any numbers of ways to build a **Bullet**. Its final construction and composition depends on its ultimate purpose.

Penetration

Bullets are designed to do damage. To do this damage, they must penetrate the target. That said – you also do not want them to damage anything other than that specific target. If a **Bullet** enters the target, damages it and then passes through the target – it is called over-penetration. And, over penetration can cause a real problem if you are engaging a threat in your home, in a mall or on the street. Remember, YOU are responsible for every **Bullet** that leaves your barrel.

Let's group our concern into two general categories: **The Range** and **The Street**.

The Range: For the majority of range time – standard ball ammunition works just fine. These are usually **Full Metal Jacketed Round Nose Bullets** – FMJ-RN. They are usually covered in a copper jacket, feed well through a semi-automatic pistol and make holes just fine.

The Shoot House: This same **Bullet**, though – the FMJ-RN – will probably NOT be allowed in a shoot house. It penetrates too well, deforms slowly and can easily ricochet off a wall or some other part of the support structure, making it a dangerous choice. This environment is where the **frangible Bullet** comes into play. It feeds well, has the touch and feel of a standard round yet will easily disintegrate upon impact with the target, (or the target trap), greatly reducing the possibility of a ricochet.

Steel Shoots: Steel shooting has become very popular over the past few years. There are some considerations here regarding the fragmentation of an FMJ-RN bullet that move it DOWN the list of desired **Bullets** and find it replaced with a **hollow point Bullet**. This is a good alternative to **frangible Bullets** due simply to cost. **Frangible ammo** is expensive – **hollow points** are not. Steel plates are typically made of AR500 or harder steel and will simply pancake any **Bullet** shot at them. However, this makes for a lot of spray as the **Bullet** is destroyed. Standard targets account for this with a down tilt of about 20 degrees, insuring the spray goes into the ground.

That said, I have still caught fragments from FMJ **Bullets** during shoots. If possible, I'd encourage you to consider **hollow points** when shooting steel; I believe it is a much safer choice.

The Street: I cannot say this enough – YOU are responsible for every **Bullet** that leaves your barrel. If you choose to carry a weapon for personal protection – you simply MUST take **Bullet penetration** into consideration when selecting your carry ammunition.

Your **Bullet** must be able to penetrate clothing and tissue. It must be able to create enough damage to change the attacker's mind to a different course of action. Or, it must be able to kill the attacker. The **Bullet** should, ideally, expend the entirety of its energy within the body cavity of your attacker and not over-penetrate, exit their body and harm the individual behind them.

To that end, the most popular **Bullet** today is the **jacketed hollow point** for your personal defensive needs. It feeds well in today's semi-automatic pistols. It has good initial penetration; it expands quickly, creating a larger wound channel; it decelerates rapidly due to this expansion, depositing the vast majority of its energy within the body cavity; and it has the lowest possibility of exiting the body and hurting people behind the attacker. There are an endless number of variations on the hollow point theme manufactured by a number of different companies. Do your research and then choose a round with a **Bullet** you are satisfied with.

Basic Shapes

There are three primary shapes for a **Bullet** – a **Round Nose (RN)**, a **Hollow Point (HP)** and a **Wad Cutter (WC)**. Then there are variations on these basic themes as well.

Bullets are defined by their **Nose**, **Body** and **Base**. Here you see a **Round Nose** – regardless of whether it is simply a lead cast **Bullet** or has a **Full Metal Jacket** round it. The **Body** is the diameter of the bore +.001 inch (typically) to enable the rifling to have its effect on the **Bullet** as it travels down the barrel. Note that there is both a **Plain Base**, meaning it is the same diameter as the **Body**, or there is a **Beveled Base** – where the edge of the **Base** is beveled slightly, allowing the **Bullet** to be seated in the case more easily. The **Nose** (or **Point**), the **Body** and the **Base** are common terms regardless of the shape of the **Bullet**. I won't take up the real estate to rehash these terms as I go through the different **Bullet** shapes.

Round Nose Bullets provide the greatest penetration and deform little unless they strike a surface significantly harder that they are. They are a poor choice for personal defense because they can easily pass through tissue. They are most commonly called FMJ and are primarily used for training, as their production costs are lower than other types of **Bullets**.

Round Nose Bullet

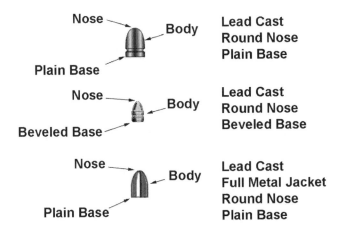

Nose — Body
Plain Base
Lead Cast
Round Nose
Plain Base

Nose — Body
Beveled Base
Lead Cast
Round Nose
Beveled Base

Nose — Body
Plain Base
Lead Cast
Full Metal Jacket
Round Nose
Plain Base

A **Flat Nose Bullet** is simply a variant of the **Round Nose Bullet** with a bit of the **Nose** taken off. This small change significantly changes the energy transfer of the **Bullet** as it passes through a body, transferring much more energy to the body cavity. This, theoretically, increases the stopping power of the **Bullet**. Still, it is a solid **Bullet** and is still prone to over penetration.

Flat Nose Bullet

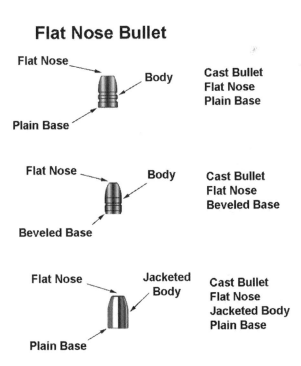

Flat Nose — Body
Plain Base
Cast Bullet
Flat Nose
Plain Base

Flat Nose — Body
Beveled Base
Cast Bullet
Flat Nose
Beveled Base

Flat Nose — Jacketed Body
Plain Base
Cast Bullet
Flat Nose
Jacketed Body
Plain Base

A **Truncated Cone** removes the rounding seen in a **Round Nose Bullet**, adds a **Flat Point** and has the same issues of over penetration that the **Round Nose Bullet** has. However, on the range it has a tendency to punch a nice clean hole rather that the tear that a **Round Nose Bullet** does. This makes it easier to score in competition.

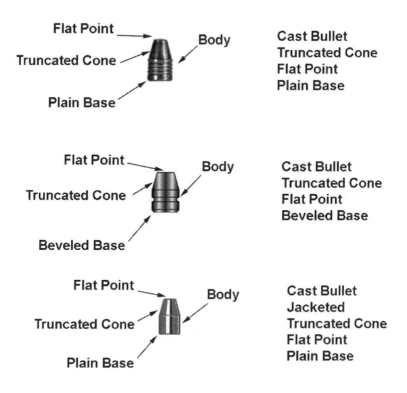

A **Wad Cutter** is simply a lead plug. Its primary purpose is for competitive shooting, insuring a crisp hole that makes for much easier scoring. However, due to this shape, it is much better suited for use in a revolver. A **Cartridge** loaded with a **Wad Cutter** would feed poorly – to say the least – in a semi-automatic pistol.

Wad Cutter Bullet

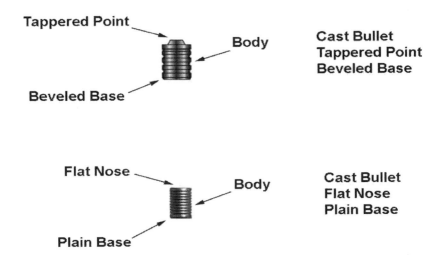

Tappered Point
Body
Beveled Base

**Cast Bullet
Tappered Point
Beveled Base**

Flat Nose
Body
Plain Base

**Cast Bullet
Flat Nose
Plain Base**

A **Semi-Wad Cutter Bullet** addresses the feeding issue. Again, its primary purpose is to insure a nice, clean hole in the target for scoring, while still feeding reliably in today's semi-automatic pistols.

Semi-Wad Cutter Bullet

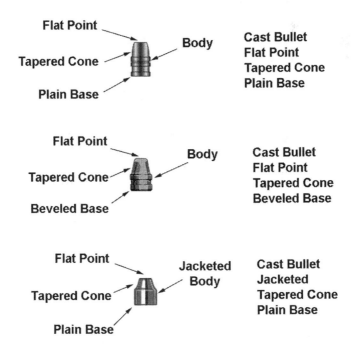

Flat Point
Body
Tapered Cone
Plain Base

**Cast Bullet
Flat Point
Tapered Cone
Plain Base**

Flat Point
Body
Tapered Cone
Beveled Base

**Cast Bullet
Flat Point
Tapered Cone
Beveled Base**

Flat Point
Jacketed Body
Tapered Cone
Plain Base

**Cast Bullet
Jacketed
Tapered Cone
Plain Base**

Hollow Point Bullet

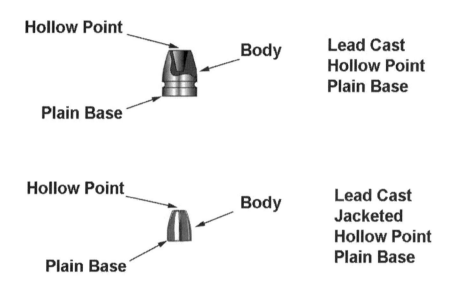

The **Hollow Point Bullet** is cast with a cavity in the center of the **Nose**. This cavity extends down into the **Body** of the **Bullet**. The idea is that as the **Bullet** enters a body, the outer edges of the **Bullet** are peeled outward, which increases the effective diameter of the **Bullet**. This does a number of things: it slows the travel of the **Bullet** through the body, it significantly expands the wound channel and it helps transfer energy from the **Bullet** to the body. These actions go a long way to reduce the probability of over penetration, keeping the **Bullet** within the body and protecting others around the attacker.

A number of new enhancements have been made to the **Hollow Point Bullet**, including some that fill the hollow with a rubber or plastic material to assist with penetration and uniform expansion. Take some time, review the alternatives and, again, choose a defensive round that works best for you.

When looking for a **Bullet** for your intended task, these are typically what you will have to choose from.

Bullet Selection

For a new shooter – let's not make it complicated.

- General range work – I'd recommend a **RN** or **FMJ Bullet**.

- Steel Shoot – I would urge you to move to a **Hollow Point**.
- Competition – try a **Semi-Wad Cutter**.

And, for personal protection – a **Jacketed Hollow Point** – **JHP** - is the round that is typically chosen. That said, a vast number of manufactures make defensive ammunition – and each has their own idea on what works best. Personally, I use Hornady's Critical Defense round. The round has a nickel plated case to reduce corrosion. The **Hollow Point** has a copper jacket and the cavity is filled with a polymer material that aids in penetration through clothing while insuring uniform expansion to increase the wound channel and to help protect against over-penetration. When choosing a defensive round – take your time, do your research, evaluate where you spend your time each day and then choose a round you believe will work best for you.

When all is said and done – it is the **Bullet** that has the final word. Make sure it's the right one for the job.

CHAPTER 3 – WHAT IS IT?
WHAT IF IT DOESN'T GO BLAM?
AND WHERE DO I CARRY IT?

WORDS HAVE SPECIFIC MEANINGS. WHEN people begin discussing the shooting community, it seems that things can go sideways pretty darn quick. Is it a gun, a handgun or a pistol? Is it a weapon? Is it a rifle, assault weapon or a carbine?

For my purposes here, there are specific differences between the use of a firearm and the use of a weapon. There are distinct types of handguns, rifles and long guns. The differences are important. The words used to describe them are important.

Sadly, weapons don't always go BLAM! when you press the trigger. Malfunctions do occur, with both the ammunition you use and the weapon in your hand. We are going to spend a bit of time talking about how to clear these malfunctions quickly and efficiently.

And finally, if you carry a weapon for personal defense, what's the best way to do that? We will spend some time covering the most common types of holsters for your weapon.

PISTOL, HANDGUN, FIREARM OR WEAPON – WHAT THE HECK IS IT?

My first exposure to handguns was with Uncle Ted and the 22. The 22 was a late 1940s Colt Woodsman. Our target was usually an array of tin cans in the sandy soil that surrounded his hand-made log cabin on a small lake in Michigan. There was little talk of safety and handling of the 22, yet his manner, respect and purpose in his handling of it loudly said that respect was due the 22 and if it didn't receive it, my shooting days would be over. I would guess my age to be twelve-ish at the time. Now, fifty-plus years later, the .22 has found a revered space in my safe. It reminds me of a man I loved and a skill he shared with me.

My father died when I was quite young, so I credit my mom with my first exposure to the world of the shotgun through an old bolt-action 410. She would hurry home from work in late fall in Michigan, we would drive to a twenty-acre woodlot we owned and get in an hour or so of rabbit and squirrel hunting before dark. In preparation for pheasant season my mom acted as the thrower, pitching pop cans down range to teach me whatever she thought she was teaching me. Looking back, it is as funny to me as it seems to be to read off the paper, yet it was done in love – she was determined the loss of my father would not interfere with my being exposed to hunting.

Years moved on and six months after the Tet Offensive I enlisted in the Air Force, July 1968. With the primary destination for many members of all branches of the services being Vietnam, all troops, regardless of their designated military skill, received some level of weapons training. And, for me, there it was – the conversion was made from the 22 or the 410 to your weapon. And thus it has remained for me – a pistol, handgun, firearm – are condensed to a weapon and all that implies.

What does the word **Weapon** actually mean? Webster's on-line defines it as:

1. **Something (as a club, knife, or gun) used to injure, defeat, or destroy**

2. **A means of contending against another**

This definition certainly fit the new skill set I was learning on the weapons range – I was learning to kill people. I'm not sure that is anything that actually can be taught. You can be desensitized to your resistance to pressing the trigger, your mind can be tricked into seeing a silhouette as a human and being conditioned to engage this threat. And yet, at that final moment, everyone has to learn that final lesson on their own. For the soldier – hesitation is death. For the civilian confronting the armed intruder – hesitation is death. Whether pistol, handgun or firearm – what you have in your hand in those instances are **Weapons**. Your knowledge, skill and willingness to employ them in your own defense determine whether you meet the next sunrise with your family or with your Maker – the choice is yours.

So where does this bring us in looking at today's training culture? There seem to be two general training communities – the NRA Community, and everyone else. Let me start with some thoughts on the NRA Community.

I am a member of this community. It is primarily oriented toward the civilian side of our society. From the Eddie Eagle to Firearms Safety in the Home to Personal Protection Outside of the Home the market and the audience are mostly civilian in nature. During training classes with Training Counselors to gain certification for various courses, one of the things stressed is the elimination of the word **Weapon** from the trainer's vocabulary. I understand the politically Correct (PC) nature of this change – heaven knows our right to bear arms is hammered enough without the NRA providing weapons training, so I get it. And I fully implement their desires when I teach their courses. In most settings, I suspect this insistence on PC vocabulary has little detrimental effect. Basic handgun, rifle and shotgun courses work fine either way, as do all the firearm safety courses. My only resistance is when we switch to the Personal Protection courses; I believe these would benefit from a change in emphasis with the use of the word **Weapon** rather than firearm. I say this with the full knowledge this will never happen, nor do I intend to push the issue with the NRA.

Bill – you're really being picky; it's just a word, for Pete's sake!

Okay, so let's look at the other training community – those who are dedicated to building your skills in using your **Weapon** to defend yourself, your family and your friends. These situations require a state of mind where you are willing to engage a threat and damage that threat up to and including killing that threat to defend yourself. As I stated earlier, this is an unnatural thing for a human to do. Contrary to the mainstream media, those of us who carry **Weapons,** those of us who have engaged in combat, do not do so out of blood-lust, but out of necessity. If you would interview soldiers, police officers or individuals who carry – not a single one would have any problem going their entire lives without bringing their **Weapon** to bear on another human being.

When I teach my Defensive Pistol classes, it is my clear intention to make sure the folks know they are stepping into a new world of responsibility and duty. They have chosen to become responsible for their own defense, to be responsible to protect their families and friends. They have realized that at two a.m., as intruders crash through their doors, the police will be minutes late to protect them; that when they grab their **Weapon,** maintain a firm grip, focus on the front sight, put it on the center mass of the intruder and press the trigger two to three times, they are using a **Weapon** to defend themselves and their families and that tremendous physical damage will be done to the intruder.

In today's litigious society I do not want my students to ever doubt what they are doing in their training or what kind of skill set they are learning – and neither should you. You are learning to use a **Weapon** capable of deadly force that you are willing to employ if you, your family or friends are placed in mortal danger.

A lot of words to say: it's a darn **Weapon** – don't beat round the bush. Accept it, embrace it, learn it.

THE SINGLE ACTION REVOLVER

The **Single Action Revolver** is a great place to begin learning about handguns. The individual parts you see labeled in the photo of this Cimarron Model P – Evil Roy signature .45 Long Colt cowboy action pistol are shared by many different types of handguns. Let's take a walk through the different parts first, and then we will discuss what makes this handgun a **Single Action Revolver**.

The chassis, the primary component that holds all the parts together, is the **Frame**.

The **Barrel** is the component that allows the bullet to exit the handgun after it is fired and adds a spin to the bullet to increase its accuracy.

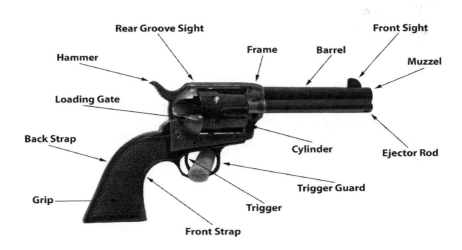

The **Muzzle** is the region immediately at the end of the Barrel where the bullet exits. used in conjunction with the **Rear Sight Groove,** is used to acquire an accurate sight picture prior to engaging a threat.

The **Hammer** is manually thumbed back to prepare it to strike the primer in the .45 Long Colt cartridge.

The **Cylinder** contains the cartridges to be fired and rotates a new cartridge into position each time the **Hammer** is thumbed back.

The **Grip** is the portion of the revolver that is actually gripped by the shooter. The **Back Strap** fits into the shooter's palm and the **Front Strap** provides a purchase for the shooter's fingers.

The **Trigger** is the component that is pressed to the rear, releasing the **Hammer** and firing the cartridge.

The **Trigger Guard** provides protection against an accidental discharge from rubbing the **Trigger** against clothing or a holster.

The revolver is loaded by opening the **Loading Gate**, pulling the **Hammer** back into half-cocked position to free the **Cylinder** and inserting a fresh cartridge, rotating the **Cylinder** and repeating this step until the **Cylinder** is fully loaded. NOTE: The **Cylinder** cannot be released and opened like a modern revolver. The **Cylinder** is ONLY removed for cleaning.

Unloading can be done by holding the **Barrel** vertical, opening the **Loading Gate**, pulling the hammer back to the half-cocked position and slowly rotating the **Cylinder,** allowing each expended round's case to drop out. In the event the case does not drop out, an **Ejector Rod** is provided to assist in this process.

The name **Single Action** comes from the fact that the **Trigger** performs a single function, to release a cocked **Hammer** to fire the cartridge. Hence, this is a **Single Action Revolver**.

This particular weapon is a lot of fun to shoot. However, as a defensive weapon it leaves a bit to be desired. The round-count in the weapon is small and the time to reload is quite long. Even cowboys back in the day had a tendency to carry two pistols rather than just one.

THE DOUBLE ACTION REVOLVER

The **Double Action Revolver** is the most common type of revolver used for personal defense. You will undoubtedly see the many common components shared between the **Double Action Revolver** and other handguns we will discuss. The weapon shown here is a **Taurus 865 .38 Special in Magnesium.** Let's take a walk through the different parts first, and then we will discuss what makes this handgun a **Double Action Revolver**.

The chassis, the primary component that holds all the parts together, is the **Frame.**

The **Barrel** is the component that allows the bullet to exit the handgun after it is fired and adds a spin to the bullet to increase its accuracy. Notice that the **Barrel** for this particular revolver is only 2.5 inches long. This affects its accuracy at longer ranges, but for typical defensive ranges – 9 to 30 feet – the accuracy is more than sufficient.

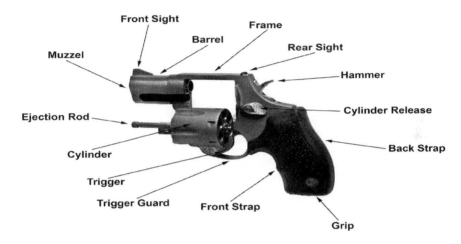

DOUBLE ACTION REVOLVER

The **Muzzle** is the region immediately at the end of the **Barrel** where the bullet exits.

The **Front Sight**, used in conjunction with the **Rear Sight**, is used to acquire an accurate sight picture prior to engaging a threat.

The **Hammer** is cocked during the process of pressing the **Trigger** to prepare it to strike the primer in the .38 Special cartridge. As the **Trigger** press continues, it breaks, releasing the **Trigger**, firing the cartridge.

The **Cylinder** contains the cartridges to be fired and rotates a new cartridge into position each time the **Trigger** is pressed or the **Hammer** is thumbed back.

The **Cylinder Release** is pushed forward to release the **Cylinder** and allows it to be pushed out of the **Frame** for easy unloading and reloading.

The **Ejection Rod** is used to eject all spent casings with a single, firm push of the rod.

The **Grip** is the portion of the revolver that is actually gripped by the shooter. The **Back Strap** fits into the shooter's palm and the **Front Strap** provides a purchase for the shooter's fingers.

The **Trigger** is the component that is pressed to the rear, rotating the

Cylinder, cocking the **Hammer** and releasing the **Hammer**, firing the cartridge.

The **Trigger Guard** provides protection against an accidental discharge from rubbing the **Trigger** against clothing or a holster.

The name **Double Action** comes from the fact that the **Trigger** is used both to cock the **Hammer** and to release a cocked **Hammer** to fire the cartridge. Hence, this is a **Double Action Revolver.** An additional function is to also rotate the **Cylinder** to present a full cylinder chamber in front of the **Barrel** prior to the **Hammer** being released.

While small revolvers like this lend themselves nicely to being concealed, they do have a tendency to have fairly sharp recoils. Also, keep in mind that to facilitate a speed reload, it's smart to have a couple of fully loaded speed loaders tucked away as backup.

There is one other version of a **Double Action Revolver** – a **Double Action Only Revolver**. As you can see by the image above, the shooter would also have the option to manually cock the **Hammer**, allowing him to fire the weapon as a **Single Action Revolver** as well.

Double Action Only Revolvers do not have exposed **Hammers**. A common example on the market today is the Ruger LCR:

RUGER LCR DOUBLE ACTION ONLY REVOLVER

Notice that the hammer is missing, requiring a full trigger press each and every time to fire the weapon.

One of the advantages to this style of revolver is that there are fewer edges to catch on clothing, pockets or the contents of a bag when the weapon is drawn.

The Single Action Semi-Automatic Pistol

Perhaps the most famous **Single Action, Semi-Automatic Pistol** on the face of the earth is the 1911 developed by John Browning and first introduced by the Colt company in – strangely enough – 1911. The move to a **Semi-Automatic Pistol** (it goes bang every time the trigger is pressed until it's empty) captured the energy of the firing of the cartridge to eject the spent casing and to feed a new cartridge into the chamber. This allowed for faster, more accurate shots as well as an expanded cartridge capacity.

Let's take a walk through this classic weapon:

The chassis, the primary component that holds all the parts together, is the **Frame**.

The **Barrel** is the component that allows the bullet to exit the handgun after it is fired and adds a spin to the bullet to increase its accuracy.

The **Muzzle** is the region immediately at the end of the **Barrel** where the bullet exits.

The **Front Sight**, used in conjunction with the **Rear Sight**, is used to acquire an accurate sight picture prior to engaging a threat.

The **Hammer** is manually thumbed back or moved into firing position by moving the **Slide** to the rear and releasing it. This prepares the **Hammer** to strike the primer in the .45 ACP (Automatic Colt Pistol) cartridges.

The **Magazine** contains the cartridges to be fired and feeds a new cartridge into the chamber each time the weapon is fired – until the magazine is empty. **Magazines** in the 1911 are typically single stack **Magazines**, meaning one cartridge is stacked directly over another cartridge in a single stack.

The **Magazine Release** is used to drop an empty magazine from the **Magazine Well** in order to make room for a replacement magazine that is fully loaded.

The **Grip** is the portion of the pistol that is actually gripped by the shooter. The **Back Strap** fits into the shooter's palm and the **Front Strap** provides a purchase for the shooter's fingers. An additional **Grip Safety** is mounted in the top portion of the **Back Strap** to provide an additional level of safety against a negligent discharge if the shooter does not have a firm grip on the pistol.

The **Thumb Safety** is mounted on the side of the weapon. Positioned up it fits into a notch on the **Slide** and insures that the **Slide** is unable to move and the **Trigger** is unable to be pressed. Positioned down, the weapon is ready to fire.

The **Trigger** is the component that is pressed to the rear, releasing the **Hammer** and firing the cartridge.

Rear Sight

Ejection Port

Slide

Front Sight

Muzzle

Hammer

Barrel

Frame

Grip Safety

Back Strap

Front Strap

Slide Lock

Magazine

Trigger

Thumb Safety

Trigger Guard

Grip

Magazine Release

Magazine Well

1911 SINGLE ACTION SEMI-AUTOMATIC PISTOL

The **Trigger Guard** provides protection against an accidental discharge from rubbing the **Trigger** against clothing or a holster.

The **Semi-Automatic Pistol** is loaded by inserting a loaded **Magazine** into the **Magazine Well** and seating it with a firm palm-slap to the bottom of the **Magazine**. The shooter than manually racks the **Slide** to the rear and releases it. This will strip a new cartridge out of the **Magazine** and load it into the chamber at the rear of the **Barrel**. From this point forward, each time the weapon is fired, part of the energy is captured to automatically force the **Slide** to the rear, eject the spent cartridge out of the **Ejection Port** and strip a new cartridge from the **Magazine** and load it into the chamber at the rear of the **Barrel**. This process will continue each time the **Trigger** is pressed until the **Magazine** is empty.

Unloading can be done by depressing the **Magazine Release** and allowing the **Magazine** to fall clear of the **Magazine Well**. To display that the weapon is empty, rack the **Slide** to the rear, ejecting any un-fired cartridge that may still be in the chamber out of the **Ejection Port**. Push the **Slide Lock** up into the notch on the **Slide**. This allows the shooter to easily verify the weapon is, indeed, empty.

The name **Single Action** comes from the fact that the **Trigger** performs a single function, to release a cocked **Hammer** to fire the cartridge. Hence, this is a **Single Action** pistol. Because the weapon captures part of the energy of a fired cartridge to activate the **Slide**, eject the spent casing and strip off a new cartridge from the **Magazine** and load it into the chamber – the only thing the shooter must do is to press the **Trigger** to fire a new round. Thus, it is a **Semi-Automatic** pistol as well.

This particular weapon has been a workhorse around the world since its introduction and continues to be a favorite for recreational shooting, competition, personal defense and as a side-arm for our military.

The Double-Action Semi-Automatic Pistol

Front Sight
Barrel
Muzzel
Slide Lock
Slide
Rear Sight
Frame
Trigger
Thumb
Safety
Back Strap
Trigger Guard
Magazine
Release
Front Strap
Grip
Magazine Well
Magazine

DOUBLE ACTION SEMI-AUTOMATIC PISTOL

Another option shooters have with **Semi-Automatic Pistols** is to purchase a version that has a **Double Action Trigger**. As in a **Double Action Revolver**, the **Trigger** performs two functions: First, it cocks the hammer and second, it releases the hammer to strike the firing pin.

In the case of a **Double Action Semi-Automatic Pistol**, racking the slide will eject a cartridge or spent casing, strip a new round from the top of the **Magazine** and drive it into the chamber. However, it will NOT cock the **Hammer**. That function is done by pressing the **Trigger** to the rear.

Let's take a walk through a **Double Action Semi-Automatic Pistol**.

The chassis, the primary component that holds all the parts together is the **Frame**.

The **Barrel** is the component that allows the bullet to exit the handgun after it is fired and adds a spin to the bullet to increase its accuracy.

The **Muzzle** is the region immediately at the end of the Barrel where the bullet exits.

The **Front Sight**, used in conjunction with the **Rear Sight**, is used to acquire an accurate sight picture prior to engaging a threat.

The **Hammer** is normally internal to the slide and not visible. The **Hammer** is manually cocked by pressing the **Trigger** to the rear. The pressure is continued until the **Trigger** breaks and the **Hammer** strikes the firing pin which, in turn, strikes the primer in the cartridge.

The **Magazine** contains the cartridges to be fired and feeds a new cartridge into chamber each time the weapon if fired – until the **Magazine** is empty.

The **Magazine Release** is used to drop an empty **Magazine** from the **Magazine Well** in order to make room for a replacement **Magazine** that is fully loaded.

The **Grip** is the portion of the pistol that is actually gripped by the shooter. The **Back Strap** fits into the shooter's palm and the **Front Strap** provides a purchase for the shooter's fingers.

The **Thumb Safety** is a mechanical device that locks the **Slide** in place and disables the firing pin. It must be manually disengaged with the shooter's thumb in order to prepare the weapon to fire. (Remember, it is a MECHANICAL device and CAN fail.).

The **Trigger** is the component that is pressed to the rear that first cocks the internal **Hammer** and then releases it to strike the firing pin, firing the cartridge. Many **Double Action Semi-Automatic Pistols** have a very stiff - and long – trigger pull. This, in many cases, takes the place of a manual or thumb safety.

The **Trigger Guard** provides protection against an accidental discharge from rubbing the **Trigger** against clothing or a holster.

The **Semi-Automatic Pistol** is loaded by inserting a loaded **Magazine** into the **Magazine Well** and seating it with a firm palm-slap to the bottom of the **Magazine**. The shooter than manually racks the **Slide** to the rear and releases it. This will strip a new cartridge out of the **Magazine** and load it into the chamber at the rear of the **Barrel**. From this point forward, each time the weapon is fired, part of the energy is captured to automatically force the slide to the rear, eject the spent cartridge out of the **Ejection Port** and to strip a new cartridge from the **Magazine** and load it into the chamber at the rear of the **Barrel**. This process will continue each time the **Trigger** is pressed until the **Magazine** is empty.

Unloading can be done by depressing the **Magazine Release** and allowing the **Magazine** to fall from the **Magazine Well**. To display that the weapon is empty, rack the **Slide** to the rear, ejecting any un-fired cartridge that may still be in the chamber out of the **Ejection Port**. Push the **Slide Lock** up into the notch on the **Slide**. This allows the shooter to easily verify the weapon is, indeed, empty.

This particular example of a **Double Action Semi-Automatic Pistol** is the Ruger LC-9. It is one of my favorite carry weapons.

There is also an additional variant to the **Double Action Only Semi-Automatic Pistol**. That is the **Double Action/Single Action Semi-Automatic Pistol**. A good example of this type of semi-automatic pistol is the CZ-75.

SINGLE ACTION/DOUBLE ACTION SEMI-AUTOMATIC PISTOL

This **Semi-Automatic Pistol** can be cocked by racking the slide to the rear. It can also be cocked by manually pulling back the hammer. And it can be cocked and fired by simply pressing the trigger. Thus it is a **SA/DA Semi-Automatic Pistol**. One advantage to this configuration would be that if you have a misfire, you can simply strike the primer one more time by pressing the trigger.

Rear Sight   Ejection Port   Slide
Front Sight
Muzzel
Back Strap
Barrel
Frame
Front Strap   Magazine

Slide Lock

Trigger
Grip
Safe-Action Safety
Trigger Guard
Magazine Release
Magazine Well

SAFE ACTION SEMI-AUTOMATIC PISTOL

The Safe-Action Semi-Automatic Pistol

Perhaps the most famous **Semi-Automatic Pistol** of modern times is the Glock pistol, first produced in 1982. The move to a **Semi-Automatic Pistol** (it goes bang every time the trigger is pressed until it's empty) captured the energy of the firing of the cartridge to eject the spent casing and to feed a new cartridge into the chamber. This allowed for faster, more accurate shots as well as an expanded cartridge capacity. The Glock pistol was the first mass-produced weapon that was made using a polymer material for much of the frame. The result was a much lighter weapon

It is called **Safe-Action** because the safety has been integrated into the very front portion of the trigger. The weapon is safe until the shooter actually places his finger on the trigger and presses the first fraction-of-an-inch to release the safety, and preparing the weapon to fire.

Let's take a walk through this latest innovation in the world of **Semi-Automatic Pistols**.

The chassis, the primary component that holds all the parts together, is the **Frame**.

The **Barrel** is the component that allows the bullet to exit the handgun after it is fired and adds a spin to the bullet to increase its accuracy.

The **Muzzle** is the region immediately at the end of the **Barrel** where the bullet exits.

The **Front Sight**, used in conjunction with the **Rear Sight**, is used to acquire an accurate sight picture prior to engaging a threat.

The **Hammer** is manually thumbed back or moved into firing position by moving the **Slide** to the rear and releasing it if the **Hammer** is internal to the slide and not visible. This prepares the **Hammer** to strike the primer in the cartridge.

The **Magazine** contains the cartridges to be fired and feeds a new cartridge into the chamber each time the weapon is fired – until the magazine is empty. **Magazines** in many Glocks are **Double Stacks**. This means that cartridges are stored nearly side-by-side. While this provides a significantly larger capacity in the **Magazine**, it does force the **Magazine** to be wider, thus increasing the overall width of the grip and the weapon itself.

The **Magazine Release** is used to drop an empty magazine from the **Magazine Well** in order to make room for a replacement **Magazine** that is fully loaded.

The **Grip** is the portion of the pistol that is actually gripped by the shooter. The **Back Strap** fits into the shooter's palm and the **Front Strap** provides a purchase for the shooter's fingers.

The **Safe-Action** safety is installed in the front of the **Trigger**. At the beginning of the trigger press, the shooter releases the **Safe-Action** safety, preparing the weapon to fire when the **Trigger** is pressed to the rear.

The **Trigger** is the component that is pressed to the rear, releasing the internal **Hammer** and firing the cartridge.

The **Trigger Guard** provides protection against an accidental discharge from rubbing the **Trigger** against clothing or a holster.

The **Semi-Automatic Pistol** is loaded by inserting a loaded **Magazine** into the **Magazine Well** and seating it with a firm palm-slap to the bottom of the **Magazine**. The shooter than manually racks the **Slide** to the rear and releases it. This will strip a new cartridge out of the **Magazine** and load it into the chamber at the rear of the **Barrel**. From this point forward, each time the weapon is fired, part of the energy is captured to automatically force the **Slide** to the rear, eject the spent cartridge out of the **Ejection Port** and to strip a new cartridge from the **Magazine** and load it into the chamber at the rear of the **Barrel**. This process will continue each time the **Trigger** is pressed until the **Magazine** is empty.

Unloading can be done by depressing the **Magazine Release** and allowing the **Magazine** to fall from the **Magazine Well**. To display that the weapon is empty, rack the **Slide** to the rear, ejecting any un-fired cartridge that may still be in the chamber out of the **Ejection Port**. Push the **Slide Lock** up into the notch on the **Slide**. This allows the shooter to easily verify the weapon is, indeed, empty.

The name **Safe- Action** comes from the fact that the **Trigger** performs as the weapon's safety as well as to release a cocked internal striker to fire the cartridge. Hence, this is a **Safe-Action Pistol**. Because the weapon captures part of the energy of a fired cartridge to activate the **Slide**, eject the spent casing and to strip off a new cartridge from the **Magazine** and load it into the chamber – the only thing the shooter must do is to press the trigger to fire a new round. Thus, it is a **Semi-Automatic Pistol** as well.

This particular weapon has been a favorite around the world since its introduction for recreational shooting, competition, personal defense and as a side-arm for our military.

Just the Basics – Magazines

Today's modern **Semi-Automatic Pistols** are typically equipped with replaceable **Magazines**. The obvious advantage is that the weapon can be quickly reloaded or a defective **Magazine** can be easily replaced. They are typically inserted into a **Mag Well** that is contained within the grip. A locking mechanism locks them into place and a **Magazine Release** allows them to fall free for easy replacement.

They typically come in two different configurations – a **Single Stack Magazine** and a **Dual Stack Magazine**.

A good example of a **Single Stack Magazine** is the **Magazine** for a standard 1911.

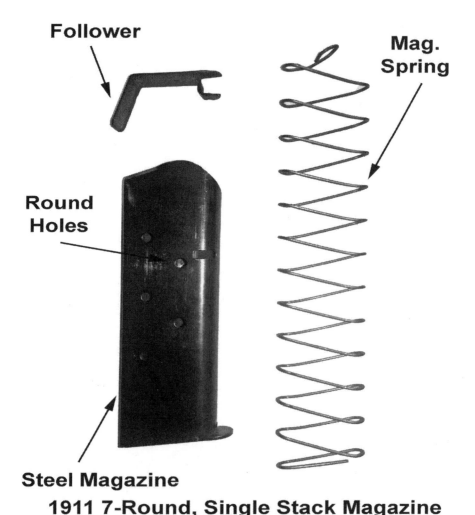

Follower

Mag. Spring

Round Holes

Steel Magazine

1911 7-Round, Single Stack Magazine

Magazines are typically made out of hardened steel. There are **Holes** along the side to show the number or cartridges that remain in the magazine. A **Magazine Spring** is inserted into the inside of the **Magazine** and pushes against the **Follower,** which is held in place by two restraining ridges at the top of the **Magazine.** These are also used to hold the cartridges in the **Magazine** until they are stripped out of the **Magazine** and loaded into the chamber by the slide going forward.

The Glock 17 **Magazine** is a good example of a **Dual-Stack Magazine**.

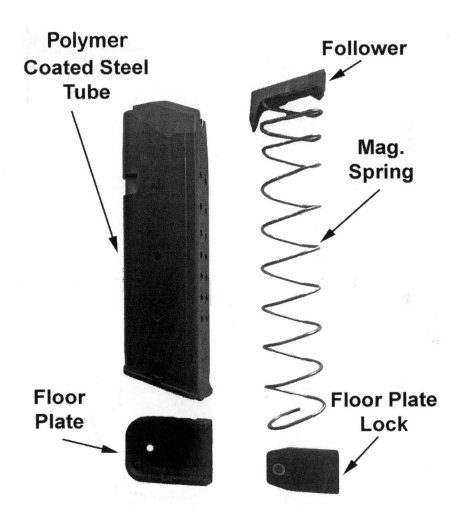

Polymer Coated Steel Tube

Follower

Mag. Spring

Floor Plate

Floor Plate Lock

Glock 17 17-Round, Dual-Stack Magazine

There are a couple differences in assembly. There is a **Floor Plate Lock** that is held in place at the bottom by the **Magazine Spring**. There is a small locking button that extends through the **Floor Plate** that locks the **Floor Plate** to the bottom of the **Polymer Coated Steel Tube**. A **Follower** is again used to push the cartridges against the top of the **Magazine**. When the weapon is fired, a new round is stripped from the **Magazine** and loaded into the chamber, readying the weapon to fire again.

Another difference is that this is a **Dual-Stack Magazine**. That means that there are two columns of cartridges in the **Magazine,** allowing for a higher capacity. This particular **Magazine** will hold a maximum of 17 rounds, compared to 7 rounds for the 1911 shown above.

Care and Feeding of Magazines

As with most things, **Magazines** like to be clean. You need to disassemble your **Magazines** periodically to remove dirt, lint and any other crap that may get trapped inside the **Magazine** during its use on the range. The absolute last thing you want is for a cartridge to fail to feed because of a small rock, chunk of lint or sand just when you are depending on that round to save your life.

These **Magazines** are your ammunition supply. Your life depends on their working well. Take care of them. Clean them, and replace them if they continually fail during your range work.

Hammers and Strikers

All cartridges fired from handguns, long guns or shotguns are fired by having their primer sharply struck by a firing pin. The mechanics to make this happen have boiled down into two primary configurations – the **Hammer-Fired** or the **Striker-Fired** firearm.

During a recent class, as I was going over this detail, eyes glazed over and I realized I had lost them and had no readily accessible images to explain this difference. I also suspect that if the folks I had in the classroom that day had questions, other folks might as well. So, let's chat a bit about **Hammers** and **Strikers**.

Let's start with one of the earliest and simplest hammer-fired weapons, the .45 Single Action Revolver.

The **Hammer** is found on the rear of the weapon. It has 4 positions:

Hammer Port

Hammer

Firing Pin Nose

Integral Firing Pin

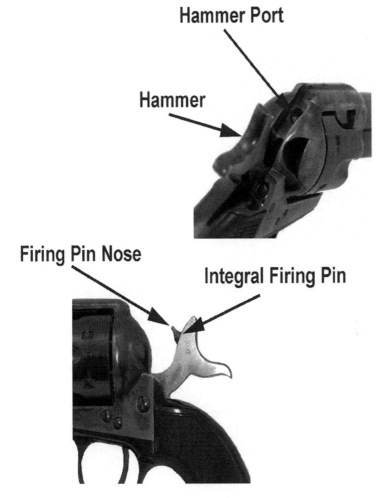

Fully Forward: The **Hammer** is fully forward, the **Firing Pin** is fully in and slightly through the **Hammer Port** – meaning it rests mere millimeters from the face of the primer of the cartridge that is in the firing position. Perhaps not the safest configuration.

Safety Position: The **Safety Position** is one-click back. In this position, the cylinder is locked, the Nose of the **Hammer** is withdrawn into the **Hammer Port**, the **Trigger** is locked and the firearm is much safer in the event it is dropped. For a modern, **Single Action Revolver**, this would be the safest way to carry the handgun – with the exception of leaving the firing chamber empty.

Half Cocked: Half Cocked is two clicks back and allows the cylinder to spin freely. This is the **Hammer** position used to both load and unload the firearm via the **Loading Gate**.

Fully Cocked: The **Hammer** is three clicks back and the weapon is fully ready to fire. In this particular **SA Revolver** – less than a pound of pressure with my trigger press will release the **Hammer** and fire the weapon.

The **Hammer** strikes the primer by plunging through the **Hammer Port**. This strike ignites the primer, which ignites the powder within the cartridge, firing the bullet down the barrel and out of the muzzle of the firearm.

The **Firing Pin** is Integral to the **Hammer,** meaning that it is a physical part of the **Hammer**. The very end of the **Firing Pin** – that part that actually strikes the primer – is called the **Nose**.

The **Single Action Revolver** evolved into a **Double Action Revolver**. This meant that by simply pressing the trigger the **Hammer** was cocked, the cylinder was rotated and finally the **Hammer** was released – firing the weapon. With this change came some changes in the design of the **Firing Pin**.

The **Firing Pin** became part of the frame. The **Firing Pin Nose** can be seen on the inside of the weapon when the cylinder is rolled open. The rear of the **Firing Pin** is available to the struck by the **Hammer Face**.

Notice that the **Hammer** has a **Transfer Bar Notch**. This provides a space for the **Transfer Bar**. This space provides a place for the **Transfer Bar** to rest when the **Hammer** is fully forward. The insertion of this bar insures that the space between the **Nose** of the **Firing Pin** and the primer is fixed, insuring that the firearm will not fire should the weapon drop. When the trigger is pressed, the **Transfer Bar** is shifted and the **Hammer Face** strikes the rear of the **Firing Pin,** discharging the weapon.

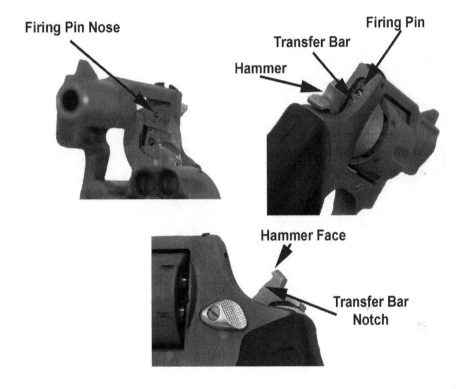

Firing Pin Nose

Firing Pin

Transfer Bar

Hammer

Hammer Face

Transfer Bar Notch

TAURUS DOUBLE ACTION HAMMER AND STRIKE FACE

The move to **Semi-Automatic Pistols** again required a change in the design of the **Firing Pin**. This Springfield 1911 is a good example of the **Hammer-FiredSemi-Automatic Pistol**.

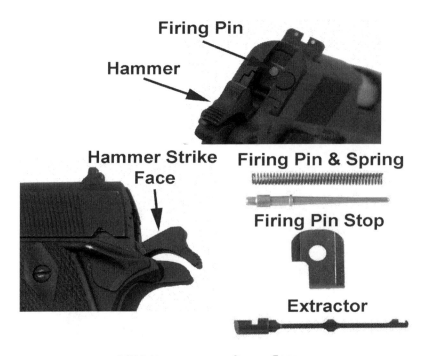

The **Firing Pin** extends slightly out of the rear of the weapon. It is pushed out by the **Firing Pin Spring**. When the trigger is pressed the **Hammer** is released and strikes the rear of the **Firing Pin**, driving it into the primer and discharging the weapon.

Notice that the **Firing Pin** is slim and tapered. The **Firing Pin Spring** is what insures that the rear of the **Firing Pin** is exposed through the hole in the **Firing Pin Stop**. The **Firing Pin Spring** is one of the components that may need to be replaced over time as it weakens and the weapon begins to experience light strikes.

The **Extractor** rides down the slide along the inner edge to slip behind the lip of the .45cal ACP cartridge. As the **Slide** moves to the rear it extracts the spent casing from the chamber and ejects it out of the side of the weapon through the ejection port.

Note that the **Firing Pin** is a fairly slender, smallish bit of hardware. This is one of the things that sets it apart from a **Striker** where the **Striker** is the **Firing Pin** – as in the Glock 36 pistol shown next.

This Glock 36 provides a good example of a **Striker-Fired** firearm. The first thing you notice is that the **Firing Pin** is significantly beefier. There is more bulk and mass to the pin. You can also see that the same goes for the **Firing Pin Spring**. It is this combination – the size and mass of the **Firing Pin** and the strength of the **Firing Pin Spring** – that will send this **Firing Pin** – the **Striker** - into the primer, discharging the weapon. There is a **Firing Pin Spacer** on the rear of the **Firing Pin** that helps to center the **Firing Pin** in its channel. The **Firing Pin Nose** will extend through the channel to strike the primer, discharging the weapon.

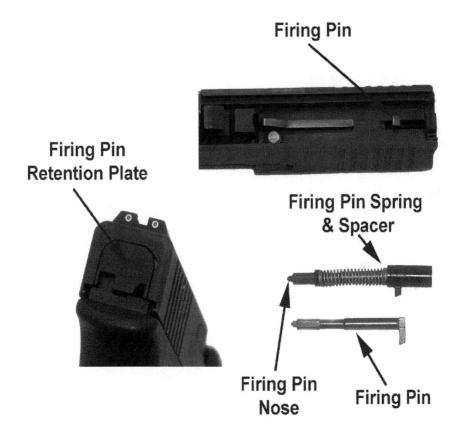

GLOCK 36 STRIKER-FIRED FIREARM

Hammers – Firing Pins – Strikers … they all get us to the same place. They make your firearm go BLAM! Yet, there are important differences.

As in all things – words matter.

And now you know that they mean …

BLAM! BLAM! Click ..... Cartridge Malfunctions

"A gentleman rarely needs a pistol, but when he does he needs it very, very badly."

–Winston Churchill

And ... it NEEDs to go BLAM!

Everything is just dandy as long as when you press the trigger your weapon goes BLAM! Yet, shoot long enough and you quickly realize that doesn't always happen. Honestly, on the range that isn't a big deal, just one more un-planned training exercise. Have it happen when a bad guy is rushing you with a knife and the whole picture changes quickly! When a malfunction happens, you need to be able to instantly respond to clear it and get your weapon back in battery. Let's chat about that a bit.

I want to cover three different categories of malfunction – **Cartridge Malfunctions, Feeding and Extraction Malfunctions** and **Weapons Malfunctions**. First I'll cover my thoughts about malfunctions in general – then focus specifically on **Cartridge Malfunctions.**

I confess to being an active voyeur of my fellow man. I love to people-watch – restaurants, airports, movie theaters, shopping malls – I love to people-watch. And, of course, on the shooting range. You see all kinds of folks. *(BTW, I realize folks watch ME as well and could easily point a finger and say Will ya look at THAT guy!)*.

There's the expert, with his/her tricked-out everything, carefully laying out his hardware on the shooting bench.

There's the newbie, doing his best just to fit in and not look silly.

There's the parent coaching the child, the husband coaching the wife, the mom coaching the daughter . . .

There's the instructor, helping anyone who will *listen. (Honestly, I need to watch this one!)*

In other words, a pretty good sampling of the human race shows up on a shooting range. Most are there to work on something – sighting in a rifle, slug gun, new pistol. They are there to practice – but not really sure just what it is they should practice. And yet, they all share one common expectation ... that when they press the trigger – their firearm should go BLAM! That does not always happen. The following process usually occurs in one fashion or another.

Shooter looks at his weapon in disbelief!

Scratches his head, racks a round or pulls the trigger again.

Hopes that it goes BLAM!

If it doesn't, or if something becomes jammed, *(said with a knowledge-able tone in his voice)*, perhaps Fred is called over, a confab is held, solutions reviewed and tried, the firearm is cleared and shooting resumes.

This hesitation, this disbelief, this calling in the expert, fosters and develops a very bad habit – a switch in focus from the 'threat meaning to send you home in a Ziploc' to 'what the hell is wrong with my gun?' This is BAD! Honestly, it doesn't matter WHY your gun stopped, only that you need to make it go BLAM! as soon as possible.

Yet, before you can really understand why the fixes work, you need to understand the failures. First, I want to focus on the **Cartridge Failures** – what they are, what they mean and how they affect the operation of your weapon.

There are three primary failures and a fourth we will chat about a bit. They are the **Misfire**, the **Hang Fire**, the **Squib Load** and a fourth – **Casing Failure**.

Misfire: A **Misfire** happens when a cartridge received a solid strike *(note I said a SOLID strike – we'll cover other types of strikes later on)* on the primer or rim of the cartridge and … nothing! Not a BLAM!, not a whisper, not a peep … nothing!

The standard response for this type of **cartridge failure** is to keep your weapon pointed in a safe direction, wait 30 seconds – then clear the round and re-engage the target. Obviously, in a defensive situation, you would clear the round immediately (or press the trigger again in the case of a revolver) and simply not wait the 30 seconds for the round to cook off.

A **Misfire**, after the primer or rim receives a solid strike from the hammer or firing pin, is virtually always due to a defective primer. While this happens with factory-loaded ammunition, honestly it is fairly rare in center-fire ammunition – and common in the much cheaper .22 rimfire ammo.

Proper disposal of Misfires: Many ranges have tubes that the **Misfires** are dropped into. Periodically either oil or saltwater is poured down the pipes and eventually the ammunition degrades. For a simple portable solution take a 20 oz. pop bottle, fill it about ½ full of water and add a healthy dose of salt to the bottle. Shake well until all the salt is dissolved. Carry this in your car or range bag. In the event of a **Misfire** – drop the offending cartridge into the bottle. Over time the salt water degrades the ammunition. You can either store these bottles or, after a year to two, find a safe spot to bury the contents.

Hangfire: You press the trigger, the cartridge receives a solid strike on the primer or rim of the cartridge and … BLAM! There is a noticeable delay from the time the primer is struck until the weapon goes BLAM! A failure of this type is usually due to a defective primer or defective powder. It is much more common in reloaded ammunition and in the black powder community.

If you have a box of factory-loaded ammo and experience a number of these at the beginning of the box, I would suggest you stop using the box and return it to the retailer. I suspect they will replace it at no cost to you in the vast majority of cases.

Squib Load: A **Squib** is a *small firework that burns with a hissing sound before exploding*.

When the cartridge receives a solid strike on the primer or the rim of the cartridge a loud hissing noise is heard that is either followed by a **muted or non-existent BLAM!** The worst-case result of a **Squib Load** is that the bullet (or shotgun wad) is left part way down the barrel. In the event the shooter fires another round without clearing the bullet or wad and insuring that the barrel is clear – a catastrophic failure of the barrel nearly always happens. This falls under my continuing mantra on the range and in the field of keeping your head in the game. If something funny happens – be aware enough to KNOW it happened and be clear on what it takes to clear the **Cartridge Malfunction**.

In the case of a **Squib Load**, you will need to empty your weapon, take a rod and insure the barrel is clear from muzzle to chamber. Failure to do this could lead to a very bad day when the next round is fired.

Case Failure: When the cartridge receives a solid strike on the primer or the rim of the cartridge the **Casing** experiences a catastrophic failure. This can look like the **Casing** splitting, the primer being blown out, the rear of the **Casing** separating, or a hole being blown in the side of the **Casing**. These types of failures seldom occur in factory-loaded ammunition. However, when a spent **Casing** is cleaned and reloaded multiple times it becomes fatigued and will eventually fail. If you do reload, carefully examine **each Casing** prior to inserting the primer and assembling the cartridge. If it looks funny – pitch it. The damage a **Case Failure** can cause is simply not worth the risk or the savings a reloaded round offers.

Cartridges are a mixture of mechanical pieces and chemical elements that depend on a specific chain of events to successfully go BLAM! As in all things, crap happens – pay attention, keep your head in the game, expect to have failures and know how to clear them.

Just because you press the trigger … there is absolutely NO GUARANTEE that it will go …

BLAM!

BLAM! … Click! Feeding and Ejection Malfunctions

Weapons that fire projectiles eat ammunition – cartridges specifically. It is beyond the scope of this chapter to cover all weapons that fit into this category. I am going to focus on the two the folks I work with have to contend with most frequently – a **Double Action Revolver** and a **Semi-Automatic Pistol**. (I don't care if it's a single action, double action or safe-action – the malfunction and its clearing process is the same.)

Double Action Revolvers: DA Revolvers are fed by a rotating cylinder. Each chamber in the cylinder holds a single cartridge. A **Failure to Feed** malfunction would imply that the cylinder or the frame is damaged enough that the cylinder can no longer rotate. In the midst of a fire-fight, where your life hangs in the balance, this is a holy crap! of the highest order and would demand immediate retreat or the rapid deployment of either a BUG (Back-Up Gun) or a secondary weapon system – knife, flashlight, tactical pen.

A **Failure to Eject**, while certainly possible, (a casing expands so much that it refuses to be ejected from a cylinder), is not a common occurrence. A very firm strike of the ejection rod is usually enough to unseat a stubborn casing. (If it does not – see the above paragraph.) If this does not result in the ejection of the empty casings, a rod can be used on each individual chamber of the cylinder until the ceased casing is found and hammered out of the chamber.

The final result ends up that clearing a **Feeding or Ejection Malfunction** in a **Double Action Revolver** is very rare and misfires are usually resolved with the simple press of the trigger to rotate the cylinder to put a fresh round in firing position.

Semi-Automatic Pistols: When dealing with a **Semi-Automatic Pistol**, there are a number of mechanical processes that must occur, in the proper sequence, for the weapon to function properly. The magazine must properly push up a new cartridge each and every time one is stripped off its top, the magazine must be properly seated in the magazine well contained in the grip of the weapon, the throat into the chamber must quickly and easily guide the cartridge into the chamber, the ejection rod must firmly grasp a spent casing for ejection, the gas from the expended round must fully cycle the slide to eject the spent casing and strip off a fresh cartridge from the magazine and jam it up the throat and into the chamber at the rear of the barrel. A failure – in any of these areas – will result in either a **Failure to Feed or a Failure to Eject**.

Failure to Feed: The overwhelming cause of a **Failure to Feed** is that the magazine is not fully seated into the magazine well contained in the grip of the weapon. The Slap portion of the Slap, Rack, Shoot clearing drill will resolve this issue. Next is a chamber throat that is full of Gun Shot Residue (GSR). This varies from weapon to weapon, but if you notice that the magazine is fully seated and the slide cycles fully, yet your next round does not fully seat in the chamber and requires a tap on the rear of the slide to put your weapon back in battery – it's a good bet a bit of scrubbing on the throat that feeds the chamber will resolve your problems.

The second, more common cure for a **Failure to Feed** is to use a different magazine. Over time they can become bent, springs can get worn and weak and they can simply get dirty. A quick magazine change will get you back in the fight quickly.

Failure to Eject: Once a round has been fired, the gas generated blows the slide rearward, the ejector rod grasps the rear of the casing, yanks it from the chamber and throws it out the ejection port. Should this fail to happen, one of two failures occurs: The empty casing remains firmly planted in the chamber of the barrel or the casing is partially ejected through the ejection port, sticking out like a stovepipe.

If the result is a stuck casing in the chamber, when the slide cycles forward again it will strip a new round off the top of the magazine and attempt to load it into the chamber. This malfunction is called a **Double Feed** and is the ONLY malfunction that cannot be cured by the Slap, Rack, Shoot clearing drill. Your cure is to:

1. Lock the slide to the rear

2. Eject the magazine

3. Rack your slide three times

4. Insert a new magazine

5. Complete the Slap, Rack, Shoot drill

The **Stovepipe failure** is typically cleared with the Slap, Rack, Shoot drill, with the hand that racks the slide sweeping the extended casing out of the ejection port. Multiple occurrences of this malfunction can be caused by a dirty weapon that results in the slide not being fully cycled. A little TLC will cure this problem.

It may be that your stance and grip is not quite firm enough and that part of the energy typically used to blow back the slide is expended in physically moving your dominant arm. This results in not enough energy being available to fully cycle the slide, and a **Stovepipe** occurs. This happens much more in today's polymer composite weapons than those that are made totally of steel. A firmer grip and a more rigid dominant arm will quickly cure this issue.

Revolvers and **Semi-Automatic Pistols** are mechanical devices. Failures happen. You will experience both **Failure to Feed** and **Failure to Eject** problems on the range and in your everyday carry. On the range – pay attention to why the failure occurred. FIX THE PROBLEM! As for everyday carry – if you are unfortunate enough to have a failure while fighting for your life – know the Slap, Rack, Shoot clearing drill. Inject problems on the range with dummy rounds loaded in your magazine or cylinder. Practice clearing these failures on each and every range visit. Carry secondary weapon systems – a knife, flashlight or tactical pen. Carry a BUG.

Because … in the real world … failure really is NOT an option.

All Things Holsters

Shooters are passionate folks. When you sit around a table with them and a few nice, cold adult beverages and talk about all things guns, there is simply no hiding these passions. Whether you talk about the best trigger, the best sight set, the best handgun, the best magazine, the best stock, the best ammunition, the best hearing protection … or the best holster, there is no lack of opinion.

Honestly, that's one of the draws for me in this community, because with passion comes a flood of information – because most true shooters are not spouting BS, but a true understanding – from their POV of course – of the topic under discussion. Listen to enough discussions and you will know these – and many other topics – from the inside out and upside down. I love that!

However, for the new shooter, this can be utterly overwhelming. While they are certainly well-meaning, if a new shooter talks to three different friends, each with their knowledge of what is the best – whatever, a new shooter ends his/her search more confused than when he/she started.

One such topic on the list of new shooters in my classes is, **What holster should I buy?** Wow, have a sit-down with virtually any shooter and ask this question and be prepared to buy more than one round as you are taught all the ins and outs of just what is the right holster. Sit with two shooters – you may as well hand the barkeep your pay check!

So, let's talk a bit about holsters, the different types, advantages and disadvantages, their purpose, and then I will share with you some choices I have made to carry the various handguns I use. Keep in mind, of course, this is all IMNSHO (In My Not So Humble Opinion).

What is its purpose?

Just what is the purpose of a **Holster**? It does a number of things.

It provides ready access to your weapon. Should the need arise, your weapon is useless if you need to open a brief case, unzip a backpack, unlock one of those spiffy fake organizers, run to a drawer, unlock a gun safe – you'll be chatting with St. Peter long before you can defend yourself. A **Holster**, worn in the same position (mostly) all the time and containing your weapon, is the first step in defending yourself, your family and friends.

A **Holster** holds your weapon securely. As you move throughout your normal day – whether sitting, standing, walking, running, bending over, crawling on your back or belly, laying on your side – it insures that your weapon isn't going to spill out of its concealed spot and go skidding across the floor, sidewalk or pavement.

Your **Holster** will protect your weapon. It protects your weapon from the bumps, scratches, gouges and nicks that would happen as you move throughout your day if you didn't have some type of protection wrapped around it. It also insures that you don't suffer from an unintended discharge because something became wrapped around the trigger.

And finally, it helps you conceal your weapon. Again, IMNSHO, I promote **Concealed Carry** – your weapon is hidden from view - as opposed to **Open Carry** – where your weapon is clearly visible on your body. It's not because I want to hide what I'm doing; I simply don't want to give up the tactical advantage I have by concealing my weapon. I know I have the right to carry under the Second Amendment – I don't need to be packin' in plain sight to prove that to myself or anyone else.

So, to recap: A **Holster** provides ready access, holds your weapon securely, protects your weapon and helps you conceal it. That is the purpose of a holster.

What types of Holsters are there?

There are a whole host of options here; we are going to talk about a few of the most common.

Outside the Waistband

The **OWB Holster** is the one most folks think of when they think of the word **Holster**. It is worn on your belt and on your dominant side – the side of your body that has the hand you will use to draw your weapon. While it is usually secured to your body by your belt, a **Paddle** can be used to allow you to easily remove your weapon while it is still in the **Holster** and then replace it later. (Honestly, I hate **Paddle Holsters** – they just never feel secure to me.)

OUTSIDE THE WAISTBAND HOLSTER

The **Paddle Holster**, is typically worn in one of two positions – the 3 o'clock, right over your hip, or the 4 o'clock, slightly behind your hip but in front of your rear pocket. The position is based on comfort, concealment and accessibility. The balance of those three considerations will decide where you wear your **Holster**.

Retention of your weapon is usually handled three different ways. First is a simple screw adjustment that is set so the weapon draws easily but is firmly retained during your normal movement.

This retention can be increased by adding a strap across the back of the weapon that first must be released before the weapon can be drawn. There are a host of designs out there – all with the intent of providing greater retention for your weapon.

The third type is a **Holster** that provides an integrated lock that must be released – typically by sliding your trigger finger alongside the **Holster** during your draw. This style **Holster** is typically worn in environments where the shooter is concerned that a bad guy may actively attempt to seize his weapon – typically in law-enforcement or military situations. Also, this style of **Holster** is usually not considered concealable – though with the right shirt or jacket that can be accomplished. One common manufacturer of this style of **Holster** is Blackhawk – their **Serpa Holster** is shown in this image.

SERPA PADDLE HOLSTER

The final type would be a simple nylon **Holster**. Typically I will use a **Holster** like this to hold a weapon within my range bag or if I am out on a backpack trip and I want something a bit more generic yet well-padded with a strap to help secure my weapon. A soft nylon **Holster** like this would typically not be used for every day carry of your weapon.

While there are certainly other options – these cover the vast majority of styles of **OWB Holsters**. The final choice for you is one of the most important you can make if you choose to carry **OWB**. It must be comfortable – you will carry your weapon all day, every day. You must be certain your weapon won't go sliding across the big box store floor the first time you bend over, and it must provide you the ability to consistently conceal your weapon with the clothing you are wearing.

Inside the Waistband

An **Inside the Waistband – IWB – Holster** fits between your pants/slacks/shorts and your body. It usually secures to your belt by either a strap or specially designed clips that latch to your belt. There are a couple of considerations to the type of **IWB Holster** that you purchase. Does it hold its form when you remove your weapon? There is added pressure placed on your **Holster** by your belt as you tighten it. While it is of little consequence while your weapon is holstered – if you draw it and then must re-holster it, if the mouth of the **Holster** collapses without the weapon in place, re-holstering can be a problem.

Second, with the weapon in such close proximity to your body, is your body protected from the sharp edges of the slide and hammer? Typically a

NYLON HOLSTER

flap of leather rises above the weapon to shield your body.

In this image you see a **Blackhawk IWB Leather Holster**. It is currently my **Holster** of choice. I wear it at the 4 o'clock position and easily forget that it is even there. The mouth is rigid enough that my weapon is easily reinserted after I have removed it from the **Holster**.

A second option that has become popular in recent years is a combination of leather and Kydex® plastic. This marries the best of both worlds – the comfort of leather against your body with the rigidity of a plastic that is formed specifically to your carry weapon. A typical example of this is one that I use made by **Comp-tac**.

I find this option to be very comfortable and again wear it at the 4 o'clock position as well.

The biggest advantage to **IWB carry** is that it is much easier to conceal your weapon. Instead of trying to cover something that may extend six inches or more below your waistband, your waistband becomes part of your concealment garment. And, while it may take some getting used to, this is a very comfortable way to carry your weapon.

BLACKHAWK INSIDE THE WAISTBAND HOLSTER

COMP-TAC INSIDE THE WAISTBAND HOLSTER

Shoulder Holsters

A **Shoulder Holster** is an assembly that is worn on the outside of your shirt. It allows a **Holster** as well as two magazines to be carried on your body. It protects your weapon, provides easy access and secure retention. Probably its biggest challenge is concealment – usually by a jacket, suit coat or sport coat. While they may look great in detective shows, everyday use can be a bit of a challenge.

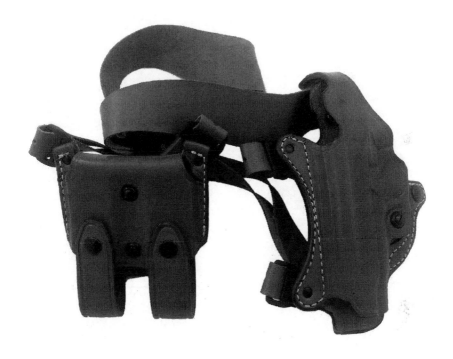

SHOULDER HOLSTER

T-Shirt Holsters

Finally, a recent addition to concealed carry, the **T-Shirt Holster**. These are undergarments that essentially have a **Shoulder Holster** integrated into their design – usually made out of a thick, soft nylon material. A pouch is provided high, under each arm that can hold either your weapon or spare magazines. I have found that this is a very flexible option for deep conceal-ment and easily integrated into a broad range of clothing. The biggest disad-vantages are that this is NOT a rapid-draw option and it can get a bit warm if worn over a very long time. Honestly, I would not wear this for every day carry, but there are situations when it is the perfect option.

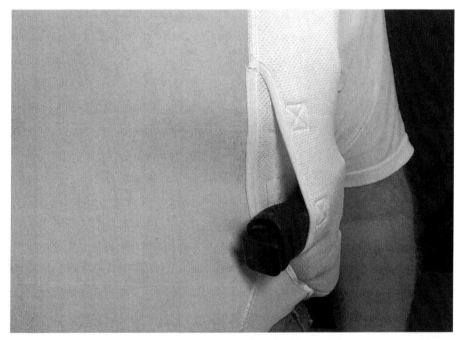

With the exception of the **Shoulder Holster**, these are my **Holster** options and ones I use every day, depending on the situation. For me – all are comfortable, secure and easily accessible.

But . . . we are all different. Take your time, choose an option that fits your lifestyle, break it in, wear it to the range, and practice with it – FREQUENTLY – and …

As I have said many times over …

Wear your darn gun! Every day!

CHAPTER 4 – BEYOND HANDGUNS

A S THEY SAY, WE ALL HAD TO START SOME-
where. That holds true for rifles as well. The earliest rifle carried was the flintlock. I believe there is a lot of value in knowing
our roots, so that is where we will start.

Long guns, carbines, tactical shotguns, survival rifles, bolt action rifles,
lever action rifles … it's a big world out there when it comes to different
weapons over and above handguns that people use for personal protection,
hunting or just plain plinking. They all have a nomenclature that is specific
to them. I want to spend a bit of time on those words so when someone
mentions a semi-automatic rifle, you'll know what it means and the common
parts that it contains.

Some of these weapons require a specific procedure for zero time on the
range to enable you to hit what you are aiming at. We're going to cover the
most common procedure to get that done.

We will spend some time on clearing malfunctions of the AR rifle platform,
probably the most common carbine platform in the US.

We will also spend a bit of time on the two most common options for
slings for the AR.

A lot to cover; let's get started.

The Flintlock Rifle

The **Flintlock Rifle** was the most advanced firearm of its time. Contrary to what most people think, they were very accurate. The **Rifle** shown here has a 60 rifled barrel firing a 50 Cal round ball with a 70 grain charge of black powder. From a bench rest position, a 4 group at 200 yards is easily achievable. These **Rifles** were the **Sniper Rifles** of the Revolution and easily outshot the smooth-bore muskets of the British Army.

The barrels were swamped, meaning that they were thicker near the breech and the muzzle. Because of the **Rifle's** length, this was done to help balance it in the shooter's hand.

You will notice components that are common on today's **Rifles** – over 200 years later.

The **Stock** provides the components to grip the **Rifle**, a **Comb** to lay against the shooter's cheek and a **Butt Plate** to rest against the shooter's shoulder.

The **Patch Box** was a compartment carved into the **Stock** to store an assortment of components needed to keep the **Rifle** in shooting condition. We will cover this separately.

The **Trigger** releases the **Hammer** of the **Lock** and the **Trigger Guard** prevents the **Trigger** from being released by passing brush and other random items.

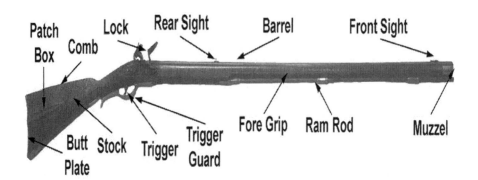

FLINTLOCK RIFLE COMPPONENTS

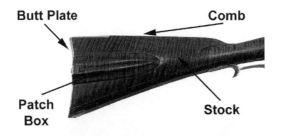

Butt Plate   Comb

Patch
Box   Stock

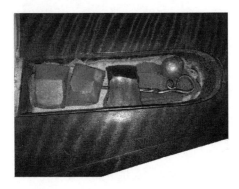

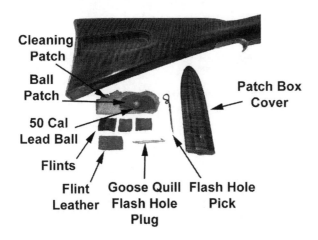

Cleaning
Patch

Ball
Patch   Patch Box
Cover

50 Cal
Lead Ball

Flints

Flint   Goose Quill   Flash Hole
Leather   Flash Hole   Pick
Plug

STOCK AND PATCH BOX

The **Rear Sight** and **Front Sight** are used to for sight alignment to insure the accurate placement of the shot. A sight radius of over four feet provided for extremely accurate shooting.

The **Barrels** were manufactured using a number of different methods. They were rifled and swamped to increase accuracy and to help balance the **Rifle** as the shooter carried it.

The **Ram Rod** was used to push the ball and patch combination down the bore of the **Barrel**.

The **Lock** is the equivalent of the **Action** in today's rifles. It will be covered separately.

Let's take a look at the contents of the **Patch Box** and the components the shooter carried with him to maintain his **Rifle**.

The **Patch Box Cover** protected the contents of the **Patch Box**. It contained an assortment of items needed to keep the **Rifle** in shooting order.

Cleaning Patches were carried to keep the barrel clean. The shooter commonly cut a **Patch**, spit on it and ran it in and out of the barrel. They used spit to prevent a buildup of powder residue at the bottom of the barrel. Spare **Ball Patches** were typically carried along with a spare **Ball** or two.

Since a **Flint** is critical to the **Rifle's** operation, spares were also carried. Each **Flint** had to be manually napped to fit the **Cock Jaws** and the **Frizzen** of the particular **Rifle**.

A spare **Flint Leather** was also carried. It's used to hold and protect the **Flint** while it is clamped by the **Cock Jaws**.

A **Flash Hole Pick** is used to clean out the **Flash Hole,** insuring the spark generated in the **Flash Pan** can penetrate all the way to the powder charge. And a **Goose Quill** was sometimes used to plug the **Flash Hole** after the **Rifle** was loaded. When the shooter was ready he would remove the **Goose Quill**, charge the **Flash Pan** and fire the **Rifle**.

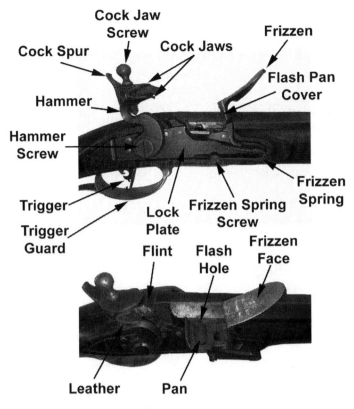

THE ACTION

The **Action** of the day was called a **Lock**. There were a number of different variations available. The one shown here is called a **Common Lock** and shares the same components that most **Locks** have.

The **Flint** is wrapped in a **Leather** strip and clamped between the **Cock Jaws**. A notch is usually cut out of the center of the fold to allow ease of adjustment of the **Cock Jaw Screw**. This is what is tightened to firmly hold the **Flint** is place. The shape of the **Flint** is napped to fit the **Cock Jaws** and to insure a solid strike against the **Frizzen Face**.

The **Frizzen** is made of steel. As **Flint** strikes steel, flecks of steel are flaked off. The energy used to do this converts the steel flakes to molten steel that is seen as sparks. The trait that allows this to happen is called **Pyrophoricity**. These sparks strike the **Flash Powder** that has been poured into the **Flash Pan,** igniting it. Note that the **Flash Pan** is curved in shape with a curved end as well. This shape helps roll the fire into the **Flash Hole,** igniting the primary charge at the bottom of the **Barrel**.

The shooter typically carried a **Powder Horn** filled with his **Primary Charge Powder** and then a separate, smaller flask that was used to pour a **Primer Charge** into the **Flash Pan**. This **Primer Powder** typically burned hotter than the **Primary Charge Powder** to help insure a solid ignition of the primary charge in the **Barrel**.

The **Frizzen** had a portion that was used as a **Flash Pan Cover**. This would allow the shooter to charge the **Flash Pan**, pull the **Frizzen** towards the **Stock,** thus placing the **Flash Pan Cover** over the **Flash Pan**. When the **Trigger** was pressed, the **Hammer** would strike the **Flint** against the **Frizzen Face**, pushing the **Frizzen** backwards, lifting the **Flash Pan Cover** and allowing the sparks to ignite the **Flash Powder**. However, attempting to charge the **Flash Pan** while it was raining, or in heavy morning dew, ran the risk of a damp charge and no ignition.

To counter this, many shooters inserted a **Goose Quill** into the **Flash Hole,** protecting the primary charge from the dampness. When he was ready to shoot he would remove the **Goose Quill**, charge the **Flash Pan** and fire his **Rifle**.

The **Frizzen Spring** applied the needed tension to firmly hold the **Flash Pan Cover** in place and provide enough resistance to the **Flint** to insure enough sparks are generated to ignite the primer charge. The **Frizzen Spring Screw** allows adjustment of this tension.

The shooter's powder was typically carried in a **Powder Horn**. These were usually made from the horn of a steer or ox. They were boiled to soften the inside so it could be removed and cleaned out to hold the powder.

The tip of the **Horn** was usually cut off and a **Throat** inserted to provide a pour **Spout**. The tip of the **Horn** was then carved to act as a cap to cover the **Throat**.

A **Base** was carved to fit into the end of the **Horn** and a **Lobe** was left to attach a **Lanyard** to the **Horn** for ease of carry.

The shooter I borrowed this **Powder Horn** from had carved a **Powder Measure** from the spike horn of a young deer. It too was boiled and a cup carved that holds exactly 70 grains of black powder. To charge his rifle he pours the powder from the **Powder Horn** into the **Powder Measure** and then pours his 70 grains of black powder down the **Barrel** of his rifle and uses the **Ram Rod** to ram his **Patch** and **Ball** into place.

In today's vernacular, this was the **Assault Weapon** of the Revolutionary War. The British were marching on the Magazine at Lexington to seize weapons like this along with their musket balls and black powder when Paul Revere made his ride. They have a rich tradition in our nation and if you ever have the chance to shoot such a **Rifle**, take some time to enjoy some of the history of our nation's earliest shooters and riflemen.

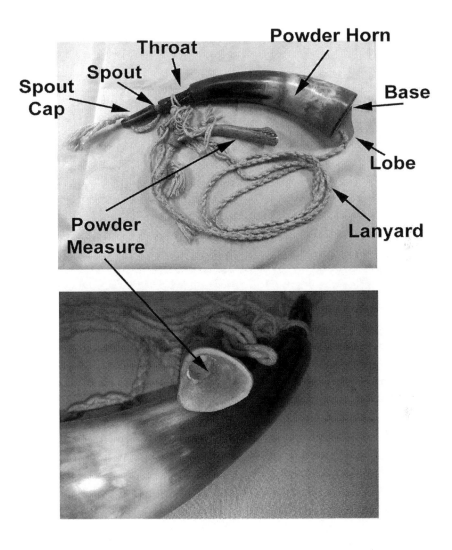

POWDER HORN COMPONENTS

The AR-15 Carbine

An introduction to a basic **AR-15 Carbine**.

The component group that consists of the **Barrel**, **Handguard** and the **Bolt Carrier Group** is the **Upper Receiver**. The component group that consists of the **Stock**, the **Grip**, **Trigger Assembly** and **Magazine Well** is the **Lower Receiver**. This is the component that is registered with the AFT as a Firearm when your weapon is registered.

The **Barrel** is the component that allows the bullet to exit the carbine after it is fired and adds a spin to the bullet to increase its accuracy.

The **Muzzle** is the region immediately at the end of the **Barrel** where the bullet exits.

The **Front Sight**, used in conjunction with the **Rear Sight,** is used to acquire an accurate sight picture prior to engaging a threat.

The **Bolt Carrier Group** consists of the **Bolt**, the **Extractor** and the **Firing Pin**. In a gas-powered carbine, a portion of the gas expelled by firing the cartridge is fed back down into a port on the front of the **Bolt Carrier Group**. The **Bolt** is driven back – ejecting the spent casing and then stripping a new cartridge off the top of the **Magazine** and driving it into the chamber. This also charges the **Firing Pin** for firing when the **Trigger** is pressed to the rear. In a piston-driven carbine a portion of the gas expelled by firing the cartridge is used to drive a piston rearward. This then drives the bolt back – ejecting the spent casing and then stripping a new cartridge off the top of the **Magazine** and driving it into the chamber. This also charges the **Firing Pin** for firing when the **Trigger** is pressed to the rear.

In the event that the **Bolt Carrier Group** fails to fully seat forward, the **Forward Assist** can be slapped with a palm to fully seat the **Bolt Carrier Group**.

The **Charging Handle** can be used to manually eject a spent casing or a malfunctioning round. Once released, the **Bolt Carrier Group** will fly forward normally.

The **Ejection Port** is the location that spent casings are eject from on the **Upper Receiver**. The **Ejection Port Cover** is provided to protect the chamber from dust and debris when the weapon is not being fired.

The **Magazine Release** is pressed inward to release the **Magazine** from the **Lower Receiver**.

The **Bolt Release** (sometimes called the Ping Pong Paddle) is activated by pressing on the paddle. This releases the **Bolt Carrier Group** and allows it to fly forward, stripping a new cartridge from the **Magazine** and seating it in the chamber.

The **Fire Selector** switches the weapon between **Safe** and **Fire** in civilian models. A **Burst** or **Auto** position is added to military and some law enforce-

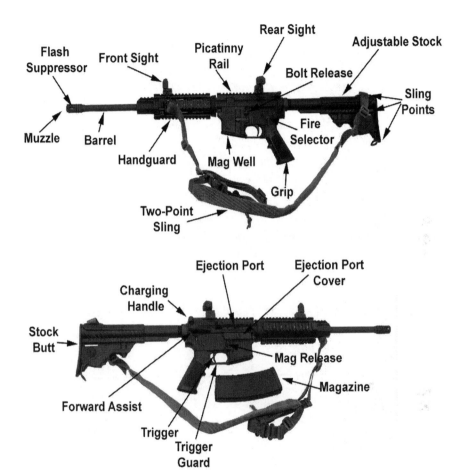

Panther Arms Oracle .223 / 5.56 16" Carbine

AR-15 Carbine Components

ment models.

The **Magazine** contains the cartridges to be fired and feeds a new cartridge into the chamber each time the weapon if fired – until the **Magazine** is empty.

The **Magazine Release** is used to drop an empty **Magazine** from the **Magazine Well** in order to make room for a replacement **Magazine** that is fully loaded.

The **Grip** is the portion of the **Lower Receiver** that is actually gripped by the shooter.

The **Trigger** is the component that is pressed to the rear, releasing the **Firing Pin** contained in the **Bolt Carrier Group** and firing the cartridge.

The **Trigger Guard** provides protection against an accidental discharge from rubbing the **Trigger** against something unexpected.

The **AR-15 Carbine** is loaded by inserting a loaded **Magazine** into the **Magazine Well** and seating it with a firm palm-slap to the bottom of the **Magazine**. The shooter than manually racks the **Charging Handle** to the rear and releases it or depresses the paddle on the **Bolt Release**. This will strip a new cartridge out of the **Magazine** and load it into the chamber at the rear of the **Barrel**. From this point forward, each time the weapon is fired, part of the energy is captured to automatically force the **Bolt Carrier Group** to the rear, eject the spent cartridge out of the **Ejection Port,** strip a new cartridge from the **Magazine** and load it into the chamber at the rear of the **Barrel**. This process will continue each time the **Trigger** is pressed until the **Magazine** is empty.

Unloading can be done by depressing the **Magazine Release** and allowing the **Magazine** to fall from the **Magazine Well**. To display that the weapon is empty, rack the **Charging Handle** to the rear, ejecting any un-fired cartridge that may still be in the chamber out of the **Ejection Port**. Push the handle of the **Bolt Carrier Release** down, locking the bolt to the rear. This allows the shooter to easily verify the weapon is, indeed, empty.

The **Stock** on most modern **AR-15 Carbines** is adjustable to establish a proper fit to the shooter for the mission and environment at hand. Also located on the **Stock** are multiple **Sling Points** used to attach a portion of a weapon sling to carry the weapon easily on the shooter's body. A **Sling** (in this case a **Two Point Sling**) is used to hang the weapon from the shooter's body. This allows them free hands to deal with whatever situation is before them.

The **Handguard** is used to protect the shooter's support hand from the massive barrel heat that is generated by firing the weapon as he grasps the weapon. The image shows a **Handguard** that is also a **Quad Rail Picatinny Rail** mounting system. These rails can be used to mount forward grips, sling points, lights, laser targeting systems as well as a host of additional attachments.

What is the difference between a **Carbine** and a **Rifle**? Well, it depends on the time period you are looking at. **Carbines** began to come into their own towards the end of the Civil War. Traditional battlefield **Rifles** were very unwieldy for mounted troops. Heavy, difficult to load, long – it was not a good mix. The advent of the **Lever Action Rifle** began during the latter half of the war. Still, these long guns, while easier to load – were still difficult to handle. Enter the **Carbine** – shorter, firing the same cartridge as the sidearm that was carried, they became the staple of the Mounted Calvary. The most famous were the generations of **Winchester Lever Action Carbines**. And that is what depicted a **Carbine** of that time period – a light **Rifle** that fired the same cartridge as the sidearm the shooter carried.

World War I saw heavy use of **Bolt Action Battlefield Rifles** and the intro-duction of the modern day machine gun – little changed in the **Carbine** arena. Fast forward to World War II and the introduction of **Garand's Battlefield Rifle**. Top loaded, rapid firing, exceptionally accurate - yet it was still heavy, bulky and slower to load than was desired. Enter the modern evolution of the **Battlefield Carbine** – the **M1 Carbine**. Shorter barrel, loaded by a bottom-fed magazine and significantly lighter. This was the pattern established in the military that is carried forward to today.

Vietnam saw the introduction of the **M-16 Battlefield Rifle**. This was compressed into the **KAR-16** and finally into today's version – the **M4 Carbine**.

So, generally, a **Carbine** fires the same cartridge as a full-sized **Battlefield Rifle** but comes with a shorter barrel; it's lighter, usually has an adjustable stock and it's equipped with the ability for equipment add-ons. A smaller, more compact weapon is much easier to handle in both urban and a wide range of field environments and has become a favorite of military organiza-tions worldwide.

Zeroing an AR-15

"What ya doin?" I ask a shooter with a brand new **AR-15** fresh out of the box.

"Sighting in my AR! Ain't she a beaute?"

She is certainly memorable: quad rail, bipod, flip-up iron sights, mounted scope, mounted flashlight with integrated laser … yep, she's a beaute.

"How's it goin'?"

"Not worth a damn … been crankin' on this optic for the past hour

and getting nowhere fast!"

"**Well, hang in there, she'll come around.**" And I quickly walk away to the 50 yard range.

It's not going to go well because he doesn't really understand what he's there for. So let's chat a bit about your next trip to the range to **Zero** your **AR-15**.

New shooters have a fondness for believing that they are **aligning their sights** with the center of the barrel so they hit the center of a distant target. MMMMmmmmm – not so much. Set aside your **AR** for a bit and let's start at the beginning – your ammunition. Just what the heck are you shootin'? And, just where do you plan to shoot it? And what is the purpose for your **AR-15**?

I teach the use of a **Carbine** as a defensive weapon. This will typically be in a CQB situation with most engagements at 50m or less, the remote possibility of a 100m engagement and very, very little chance of a weapon being employed in a defensive situation with the threat being more than 100m away.

Next, what round are you going to be using? The standard NATO 5.56 round has a muzzle velocity of 3020 fps and has a bullet weight of 62gr. As soon as the bullet leaves the barrel, gravity begins acting on it (let's leave wind out of the formula here, that's a discussion for another time). And your bullet will begin to drop. The charts for an American Eagle AE223N (a civilian approximation of a standard NATO 5.56 round) are as follows:

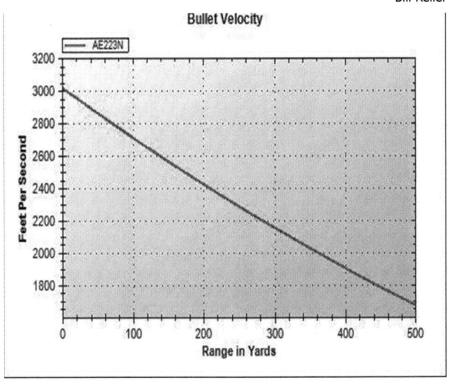

The bullet trajectory chart looks like this:

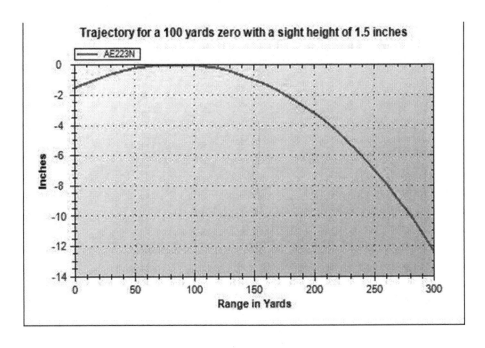

Just what do these charts mean? First, the bullet bleeds velocity quickly. Within the first 100m the bullet has lost around 300fps. However, over 200 yards the round is fairly flat with the round being approximately 3 inches below the zero point at 200 yards.

Let's compare these characteristics with the AE223 round that I bought in a 1,000 round brick this past week. The AE223 is a slightly faster round with a 55gr bullet and its characteristics look like this:

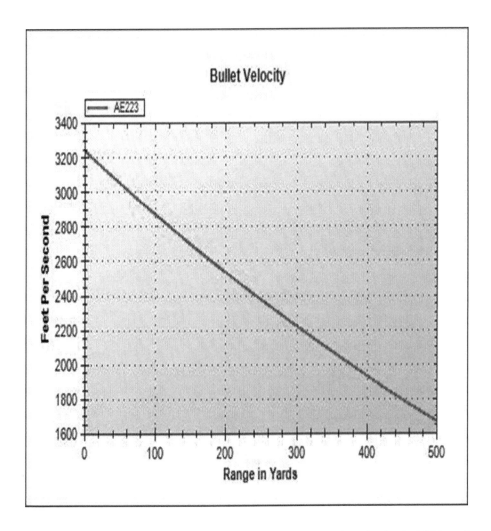

While the speed drops here as well, the initial muzzle velocity is 3250 and nearly 2900fps at 100m. The trajectory is a bit flatter when compared to the AE223N;

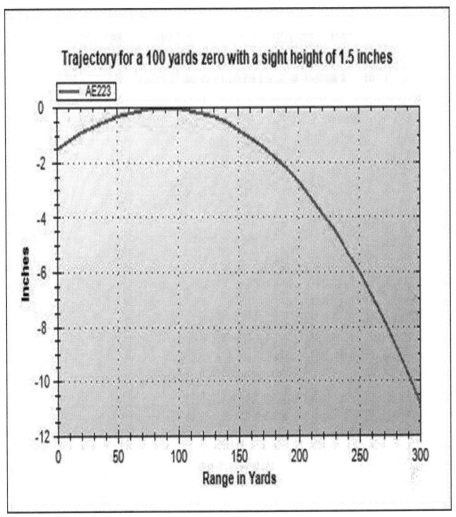

The bullet drops only 2.5 inches over 200m from the 100m zero.

Fine, fine – charts, math, yadda, yadda – just what are we **Zeroing** here anyway?

OK, we are using our weapon at a distance that will typically be 100m or less. For me, I was using a AE223 round. I wanted it to be **Zeroed** at 100m. This will give me a weapon that will hit within 3 inches of center between 0-200m. More than effective for any threat I may encounter.

You will note from the trajectory chart that when the bullet leaves the muzzle it begins to climb. For a weapon **Zeroed** for 100m, it is at that distance that your bullet will kiss the center of your target. Once past the 100m point, the bullet begins to drop and is about 2.5 inches below center at 200m.

When you are **Zeroing** your weapon, you are **setting your Sights** (iron in my case) such that you are compensating for the flight of the bullet so that, at your chosen distance, there is **Zero** drop and you hit the center of your target. Note that if you would decide to **Zero** at 200m, or 300m your **Sight** would need to be adjusted accordingly.

The same goes for your bullet as well – heavier bullets, faster drop, lower velocity – all of which affect your impact point.

So, we have chosen our optimal fighting distance – 100m. We have chosen our ammunition – AE223. And we have chosen our sighting system – **Iron Sights** with a **Post Front Sight** and a small diameter **Rear Peep Sight**. Let's get started.

Next, select a **ZeroTarget** for the range at which you want to **Zero**. You can find them on the **www.ar15.com** website at this **link**. Note that they acknowledge the different types of rounds. These targets will get you very close, with some final tweaking being needed for your specific ammunition once you are essentially on target. Note that these are 25m targets – and will save you a lot of walking time back and forth down range, especially if you are **Zeroing** for longer distances – 200m or 300m.

Set the **Base Plate** for the **Front Post** level with the bottom of the **Notch** on your front sight. This is done by depressing the **Locking Post** on your **Front Sight** and turning the **Base Plate** indicated by the location of your round hit. You will need to move it either up or down.

AR-15 FRONT SIGHT   AR-15 REAR SIGHT

For the **Rear Sight**, the starting point is the center of the hole in the **Peep Sight** being aligned with the center of the **Rear Sight.** This may be facilitated by gradients being etched on the sight or by simply counting the number of clicks it takes for the **Peep Hole** to traverse the **Rear Sight**. Then, divide the number of clicks by two and then set the **Peep Sight** to the center of the **Rear Sight**.

You are now ready for your first 3-round group. Find the center of the group and adjust accordingly, based on the location of the hits and the instructions on your **Zero Target**. Here is my alignment target and my groups:

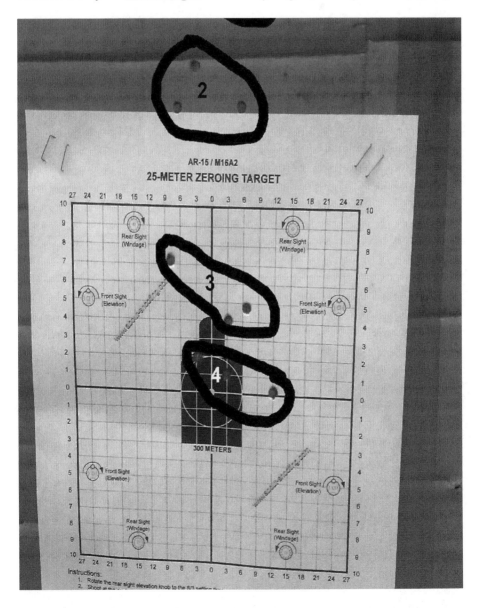

My first 3-round group was well above the target. 3-clicks CCW brought it down to #2, 6-clicks CCW brought it down to #3 and another 3 clicks CCW brought it down to #4. I had 1 flyer in #3 group and 1 flyer in #4 group, which I simply ignored. Notice that there were no adjustments needed for windage (left/right adjustment).

My **Zeroing** for 100m is complete.

I did use a bench rest shooting position for this adjustment. On our range, I used a portable table set at the 75ft line for this alignment. Here is what the shooting position looked like:

BENCH REST SHOOTING POSITION

So, how did the puppy shoot after this? Well the boy and I did some cognition drills – your shooting buddy calls out target and round count and initiates your round by a command like SHOOT or FIGHT and you engage the targets in the order specified. Here is my first drill with my new **Zeroed AR-15**:

NOTE TO SELF – when you set your **Zero** for **Point Of Aim** – don't use 6 o'clock when you engage your target. Heavy sigh … head in the game, head in the game …

We shot a number of cognition drills checking for consistent groups, whether the sights remained firmly attached to the rails and just general weapon operation. I was more than pleased with the results.

So there you go. **Zeroing** your **AR-15** platform isn't rocket science. Still, you have to be aware of what you are doing, why you are doing it, and have a known, consistent process to get a solid final result. Give this a try the next time you go to the range to **Zero** your **AR-15**.

REMINGTON 870 TACTICAL SHOTGUN

A **Shotgun** is an excellent close-quarter defensive weapon. It provides solid fire power, it's less dependent on an accurate sight picture and it can present a frightening threat to an attacker.

It can handle a wide array of munitions – from a highly accurate rifled slug typically weighing 1 ounce to bird shot. Options can also include buckshot and a full range of shotgun BB sizes as well. While it is tempting to go with a slug or buckshot for defensive ammunition in your home, lighter weight shot between 5 and 7 provides good deterrence but much less risk of penetration of your home's walls. This can do a great deal to protect family members who may be taking cover or concealment in other rooms.

When the word **Tactical** is wedded to the name, the implication is that the weapon is primarily designed as either a defensive or offensive weapon to be used against a human threat. Typically they are outfitted with pistol grips, augmented alignment system, perhaps a collapsible stock, and picatinny rail systems to mount lights, lasers or additional fore-grips. The **Remington 870 Tactical Shotgun** shown is my personal **Tactical Shotgun** and is a very basic model.

The basic components of the **Shotgun** are as follows:

Remington Model 870 Tactial 12 ga. Shotgun

The **Butt Plate** rests against the shooter's shoulder. It may be replaced by a **Recoil Pad** to lessen the effect of the shotgun's recoil on the shooter's body.

The **Stock** provides three major weld points to the shooter's body; The **Comb** is welded to the shooter's cheek, the **Butt Plate** to the shooter's shoulder and the **Pistol Grip** is firmly grasped by the shooter's dominant hand.

The **Trigger** releases the **Firing Pin** and fires the round contained in the shotgun's chamber. The **Trigger Guard** protects the **Trigger** from accidental discharges due bumping against brush, clothing or other items in the area. The **Safety** prevents the **Trigger** from being pressed to the rear unless it has been released by the shooter. (**NOTE: Safeties are mechanical devices and can fail!**)

The **Action Bar Release**, when depressed, allows the **Fore-End** to move to the rear. This is typically activated to allow the **Fore-End** to be repeatedly operated to unload the shotgun.

The **Loading Port** provides the ability to load shotgun shells into the **Tubular Magazine**.

The **Sling Point** provides a connection point for a **Sling**.

The **Muzzle** is the region in the immediate area at the front of the **Barrel**.

The **Barrel** provides form and shape to the pattern off the shot as it leaves the **Barrel**. It may also be rifled to provide spin to a slug, increasing both its accuracy and its range; or choked to provide different spread options for shot loads.

The **Front Bead** acts as the front sight of a shotgun. The shooter's eye acts as the rear sight when his cheek is firmly welded to the comb and the shooter is looking down the **Barrel** to the **Front Bead**. **Tactical Shotguns** may also use traditional **Front Sights** and **Flip-Up Rear Sights** or even a **Red-Dot Sight**.

The **Barrel Guide Ring** provides proper spacing between the **Barrel** and the **Tubular Magazine** and holds both rigid, allowing easy use of the **Pump Action** of the **Fore-End** to eject spent hulls or to load a new shotgun shell into the chamber.

The **Ejection Port** provides an opening that allows the spent hull to be ejected, making room for a new shell.

The **Remington Model 870** is a **Pump Action** shotgun. The **Fore-End** is pumped to the rear – this opens the **Ejection Port**, removes a shell from the **Tubular Magazine** and places it in the breech (the region exposed when the **Ejection Port** is opened). Pumping the **Fore-End** forward closes the **Ejection Port**, forces the shell into the chamber at the rear of the **Barrel** and cocks the **Firing Pin** in preparation for firing. The **Pump Shotgun** must be pumped between each round that is fired until the **Tubular Magazine** is empty.

The Springfield Armory M6 Scout Survival Rifle / Shotgun

When you talk about a true **Survival Rifle** you enter an entirely different realm. These are weapons of last resort – never really meant to be used but, when they are required, they must be 100% reliable. This implies a number of characteristics that set them apart from a standard TSHTF weapon.

- Minimal moving parts
- Extreme durability
- Simple operation
- Exceptionally reliable

One of the icons of this class of weapon is the **Springfield Armory M6 Scout Survival Rifle**.

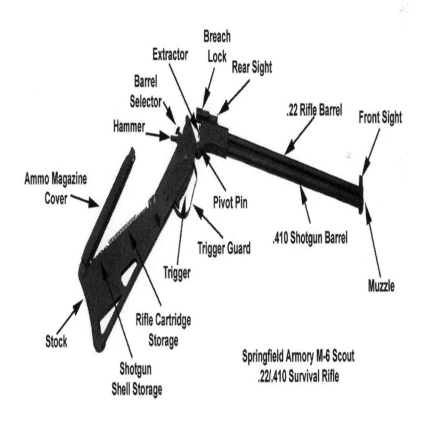

SPRINGFIELD ARMORY M-6 COMPONENTS

The **M6** was a standard component of survival kits for Air Force aircrews beginning in the 1950s through the early 1970s. It is a beast. Weighing in at nearly 5 pounds, it is 34 inches long when assembled. The upper barrel is either chambered for a .22LR or a .22 Hornet round. The lower barrel is chambered for a .410 shotgun shell.

The **Hammer** is manually cocked, the **Barrel** is manually selected and an oversized **Trigger** accommodates easy firing – even with a gloved hand.

An ammo **Magazine** built into the **Stock**, and secured by a locking cover, holds an emergency supply of .410 shells and .22 cartridges.

If you are looking for a last-ditch **Survival Weapon**, the **M6** should be at the top of your list!

The **Rifle Barrel** is the component that allows the bullet to exit the **Carbine** after it is fired and adds a spin to the bullet to increase its accuracy. The **Shotgun Barrel** channels and patterns the shot expelled from the .410 shotgun shells.

The **Muzzle** is the region immediately at the end of the **Barrel** where the bullet exits.

The **Front Sight**, used in conjunction with the **Rear Sight** is used to acquire an accurate sight picture prior to engaging a threat or taking game.

The **Trigger** is the component that releases the **Firing Pin**.

The **Trigger Guard** is provided to protect the shooter from an unintended discharge due to clothing, brush or other item the **Trigger** may bump against.

The **Hammer** is manually cocked, preparing the weapon to fire. The **Barrel Selector** is used to select which **Barrel** will be fired when the **Trigger** is pressed.

The **Ejector** removes the spent cartridges when the **Breach Lock** is lifted and the weapon is broken open. The **Pivot Pin** is used to assemble the **Stock Group** and **Barrel Group** into a full sized weapon. These may be disassembled for easy storage in your survival kit.

This is a highly accurate weapon allowing the shooting of small game to 50 yards and beyond. As a defensive weapon, while better than nothing, its slow rate of fire would make it a less than optimal weapon. However, it would make sense to include a couple .410 slug rounds as part of the ammo **Magazine's** cache of ammunition.

These weapons have a long, proud history and are well worth adding to any survival kit.

Winchester 94 .45 L/C Saddle Gun Carbine

The **Lever Action Carbine** is one of the iconic weapons of the Old West. This is my .45 Cal **Long Colt Saddle Gun**. It is fun to shoot, carries a full 10 rounds and is very accurate out to 50 yards. Past that needs a little practice for Kentucky windage .

The advantage for the settler who carried both a **Colt Single Action** and a **Colt Lever Action Carbine** is that they both shot the same round. That put a sizable amount of fire power in the hands of a skilled shooter.

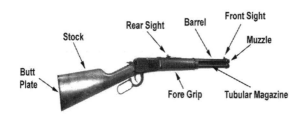

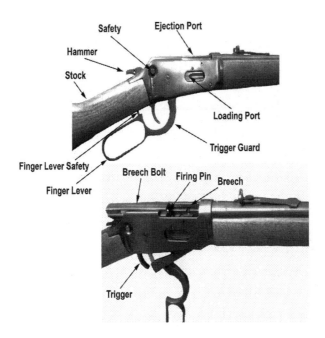

Winchester 94 .45cal L/C 16" Saddle Gun Carbine

The **Barrel** is the component that allows the bullet to exit the **Carbine** after it is fired and adds a spin to the bullet to increase its accuracy.

The **Muzzle** is the region immediately at the end of the **Barrel** where the bullet exits.

The **Front Sight**, used in conjunction with the **Rear Sight,** is used to acquire an accurate sight picture prior to engaging a threat.

The **Fore Grip** provides an area for the shooter to grasp the front portion of the weapon to assist in steadying if for an accurate shot.

The **Tubular Magazine** contains the cartridges to be fired and feeds a new cartridge into the chamber each time the **Finger Lever** is operated until the **Magazine** is empty.

The **Finger Lever** is the mechanical component used to eject expended casings from the weapon and push a new round into the chamber.

The **Finger Lever Safety** requires the shooter to firmly grasp the **Finger Level** and the **Stock** to enable the trigger.

The **Breech** is the area of the weapon where an expended cartridge begins its exit from the weapon and a new cartridge is placed before it is rammed into the chamber.

The **Breech Bolt** acts as the ejection tool to remove a spent casing, the ram to insert a new cartridge into the chamber. It contains the **Firing Pin**, which will fire the cartridge when the **Trigger** is pressed and it is part of the containment system to contain the energy of the cartridge and help force its gasses down the **Barrel** and out the **Muzzle**.

The **Finger Lever** is the component that harnesses the work done by the shooter's hand and allows him to expel an expended cartridge and ram a new cartridge into the chamber.

The **Trigger** is the component that releases the **Firing Pin**.

The **Trigger Guard** is provided to protect the shooter from an unintended discharge due to clothing, brush or other item the **Trigger** may bump against.

This particular weapon has dual **Safeties** – one just rear of the **Breech Bolt** and one between the **Finger Lever** and the **Stock**. The lever must be gripped and the **Safety** released for the weapon to fire.

The **Stock** attaches to the rear of the **Receiver** and the **Barrel** with a **Tubular Magazine** (for this particular weapon) attaches to the front of the **Receiver**. The **Stock Butt Plate** firmly rests against the shooter's shoulder while the weapon if fired.

The advent of the **Carbine** in the late 1800s provided a person an accurate, longer range weapon, easily carried and handled on horseback that typically used the same cartridge as his sidearm. Is it any wonder it remains a popular firearm nearly 120 years later?

The Bolt Action Rifle

For many shooters, the **Bolt Action Rifle** is the pinnacle of development for accurate shooting. Many of the most popular **Military Sniper Rifles** continue to be made in a **Bolt Action** format. While the rate of fire is slower than a **Semi-Automatic Rifle**, these shooters are confident in their belief that the **Manual Bolt Assembly** can do a more consistent job of seating the next round than a **Semi-Automatic Action**.

A **Bolt Action Rifles** with a mounted **Scope** comes with its own set of unique nomenclature.

The **Barrel** is the component that allows the bullet to exit the **Carbine** after it is fired and adds a spin to the bullet to increase its accuracy.

The **Muzzle** is the region immediately at the end of the **Barrel** where the bullet exits.

The **Fore Grip** provides an area for the shooter to grasp the front portion of the weapon to assist in steadying if for a sturdy shot.

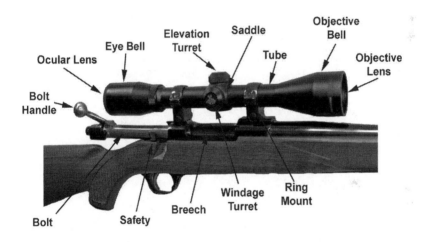

Ruger M77 7mm Bolt Action Rifle

BOLT ACTION RIFLE COMPONENTS

The **Breech** provides a **Port** for loading the **Magazine** with fresh cartridges as well as acting as the **Ejection Port** while working the **Bolt** to eject a spent cartridge.

The **Bolt** acts as the ejection tool to remove a spent casing, the **Ram** to insert a new cartridge into the chamber; it contains the **Firing Pin**, which will fire the cartridge when the **Trigger** is pressed and it is part of the containment system to contain the energy of the cartridge and help force its gasses down the **Barrel** and out the **Muzzle**. The **Bolt** is manipulated by using the **Bolt Handle**. The **Bolt Handle** is lifted and the **Bolt** is moved to the rear. This ejects a spent cartridge from the chamber. The **Bolt** is then shoved forward, stripping a new cartridge from the **Magazine** and inserting it into the chamber. The **Bolt** is then pushed down, locking the **Bolt** in place.

The **Trigger** is the component that releases the **Firing Pin**.

The **Trigger Guard** is provided to protect the shooter from an unintended discharge due to clothing, brush or other item the **Trigger** may bump against.

The **Stock** provides three major weld points to the shooter's body; The **Comb** is welded to the shooter's cheek, the **Butt Plate** to the shooter's shoulder and the **Grip** is firmly grasped by the shooter's dominant hand.

Also located on the **Stock** are a **Front Sling Point** and a **Rear Sling Point** used to attach a portion of a weapon **Sling** to carry the weapon easily on the shooter's body. A **Sling** – typically a **Two Point Sling** - is used to hang the weapon from the shooter's body.

The **Safety** prevents the **Trigger** from being pressed to the rear unless it has been released by the shooter. (**NOTE: Safeties are mechanical devices and can fail! Safeties may also be located in different positions relative to the Bolt.**)

This particular configuration of the **Ruger M77** incorporates a **Telescopic Site** to provide a solid sight picture at extended distances. Like any device, it has a specific set of vocabulary to describe its different components.

The **Ocular Lens** is that lens group that is closest to the shooter's eye. The **Eye Bell** is the housing that contains the **Ocular Lens** group.

The **Elevation Turret** is used to adjust the bullet's impact point either up or down. The **Windage Turret** is used to adjust the bullet's impact point either left or right. A **Saddle** is used to marry these two adjustment groups together on the **Scope**.

An **Object Lens** group is contained in the **Objective Bell** and is at the front end of the **Scope**. A **Tube** connects the **Eye Bell** to the **Objective Bell**. **Mounting Rings** hold the **Tube** in place and mount it to the top of the **Rifle**.

If you have never shot a **Bolt Action Rifle**, take some time to do so. There is a rhythm, a smoothness to the process that I believe you would come to enjoy.

The Sling

When you start a discussion about **Rifle Slings**, you are sure to hit more than a few hot buttons in the shooting community. However, past the specific manufacturer, the specific connector system, the specific material – there are basics about a **Sling** that every new shooter should be aware of. And that is what I would like to spend some time on.

First – let's divide **Slings** into two general categories – **Combat Slings** and **Precision Shooting Slings**. In each of these two environments there is overlap of purpose. But the primary purpose of a **Sling** in combat differs significantly from the primary purpose of a **Sling** for precision shooting. First, we will take a walk through **Combat Slings**.

Combat Slings

Purpose: There are three primary purposes for a **Sling** in combat – weapon retention, weapon transition and load distribution.

Weapon Retention: In the heat of battle, losing your primary battle weapon is not a good thing. This may happen by simply dropping it while traversing a stream or a steep mountain trail, or it may happen during a close encounter with an enemy who may well try to seize your weapon. A **Sling** will help to secure your weapon to your body in insure it is not lost . **Retention** can also apply to physically securing it closer to your body in the event you need your hands to climb, or you need to pick up a fallen buddy or for any other reason where you need free hands and you don't want your battle **Rifle** banging around your body.

Weapon Transition: In the heat of battle you hear a deafening click … and you need to **Transition** to a secondary weapon – sidearm, knife, fists. By simply letting go of your battle weapon your hands are free to **Transition** to the secondary weapon system. And, when the moment passes, and you have time to repair the weapon malfunction – you will know exactly where your weapon is.

Load Distribution: During an extended patrol, everything begins to weigh more – including your battle weapon. A **Sling** helps distribute part of the weight over a wider amount of your body rather than simply two hands/arms that are tasked with carrying it.

There are two primary variations of the **Combat Sling** – a **Two Point Sling** and a **Single Point Sling**. While there are multiple variations on these two themes, each has primary characteristics.

Two Point Sling: The **Sling** attaches to two separate **Sling Points** on your weapon. One is usually near the rear of the stock and the second somewhere on the fore-grip. My personal preference is the **Vickers padded**

Two Point Sling. It allows for easy adjustment whether I want to snug my weapon to my body during movement or if I want to extend and engage with my weapon. The biggest advantage to a **Two-Point Sling** is that when both hands are needed, the weapon can be drawn close to your body so that as you move your hands are free yet your weapon doesn't bounce off your thighs and knees.

Single Point Sling: A **Single Point Sling** is attached to a single point on your weapon. This is typically to a ring located near the top of the mag well or forward of the stock. It typically has a shock cord feel so that while you can keep your weapon close to your body, it easily stretches during engagement without the need for additional adjustments. The biggest fault I find with a **Single Point Sling** is the amount of movement of the weapon when it is released to hang free on your body. If you do this during movement, you are guaranteed some pretty good-sized bruises by the end of the day.

Another big area discussion is, "How the heck do I wear this darn thing?" Honestly, to me it's as clear as day. You want easy access to your secondary weapon system. This is typically a handgun worn on your dominant hand side – therefore, I want that arm to have the most movement possible. I wear either of these **Slings** by putting my head and SUPPORT arm through the hole. This insures that there are no obstructions on my dominant side between me and my secondary weapon system.

Precision Shooting Sling

Probably the most famous **Precision Shooting Sling** is the **M107**. There are a number of crossover characteristics between the **M107** and **Combat Two Point Slings**. Both are **Two Point Slings**. Both will keep your weapon close to your body during movement. While both are adjustable, the **M107** does take a significant amount work compared to many modern **Two Point Slings**.

Where the **M107** excels is in providing a significantly improved and more stable shooting platform. While typically limited to either the kneeling or sitting shooting position, the **M107** allows an additional point of contact to help secure and stabilize your shooting platform. This is formed through the use of a **Lower Keeper** and the **Long Strap** to form a loop that fits around your support arm bicep. The length of these two elements is adjusted such that, when your support arm bicep rests on your knee, your weapon is drawn into your knee, helping to secure it. Through this additional point of contact with your body and the use of your knee as a resting place for the lower part of your bicep, your shooting platform becomes much more stable, allowing for more accurate, long range shots.

There was an excellent article on the M107 written for the Shooters Carnival in October of 2003. Follow the link to read this excellent article.

http://carnival.saysuncle.com/001086.html#001086

Slings are a vital part of your **Battlefield Rifle/Carbine**. Find one that you like and fits you well. Then work with it, use it, train with it.

CHAPTER 5 – SHOOTING A HANDGUN

SHOOTING A HANDGUN WELL IS A COMBINATION of any number of details – individual acts that you must get right each and every time.

Your body has chosen a hand and an eye it would prefer you use to shoot your handgun. Which eye is dominant for you?

Shooting well begins with your foundation – your stance. Where you place your feet and hold your body. Then it depends on your having a firm grip on your weapon. It requires that you have good sight alignment and have a good sight picture. Your breathing enters into the picture while you are pressing the trigger straight to the rear.

There's much to consider when you are trying to get rounds on a target or rounds on a threat intent on doing you harm.

In a defensive situation, time is of the essence. What's the fastest way to get rounds on your threat? Metal on Metal.

GET A GRIP

There are many pieces to the puzzle of a shooter being able to get hits on a target or a threat with a handgun – all equally important. However, there is one that acts as a foundation for all the others, their **Grip** .

A proper **Grip** will weld your weapon to your body – it fully integrates it into your overall structure. It becomes an extension of your hand, your arm, your body. When done properly, your **Grip** transfers the stability of your body to the weapon and then channels the recoil of firing your weapon throughout your body. The final result of such a **Grip** is that accurate shots can be delivered quickly to knock down the threat. There are three primary elements to a proper **Grip**: it should feel natural, it should be consistent and it should be firm

It should feel natural.

Many elements that go into a natural feel, and they all contribute to "This just doesn't feel right in my hand" or "I love how it fits me" style comments. The overall shape of the **Grip** is a large component. Early handguns had a tendency to be thick and round, more like the common hand tools of the time – a shovel, axe, hammer, buck saw – tools that felt familiar to the user. The disadvantage to this style was that it didn't always properly channel the recoil into a shooter's body. Of course early handguns were typically only fired once in a fight; the battle then continued with some kind of edged weapon – cutlass, foil, rapier or some other type of sword.

With the advent of a repeating handgun – beginning with the black powder pistol and continuing through today's modern double action revolvers – the ability to fire multiple shots quickly meant that recoil needed to be managed more effectively to insure accurate follow-up shots. To help in this effort, the **Grips** of revolvers changed shape to better fit a shooter's hand. They became a bit thicker front strap to back strap and a bit narrower in width. The curve of the **Grip** became better fitted to the space created between the palm of the hand and the large pad of the palm beneath the dominant hand's thumb. These modifications allowed the recoil to be channeled from the rear of the chamber through the **Grip** and into the centerline of a shooter's extended arm. By using the **Grip** to weld the handgun to the shooter's body, the entire mass of the shooter could now be brought to bear in controlling recoil. This allowed the shooter to deliver quick and accurate fire on a threat – at least until the weapon was empty.

With the advent of **John Browning's 1911** a new element entered the vernacular – **Grip Angle** . This is the **Angle** at which the centerline of the **Grip** is tipped forward toward the muzzle from the vertical. You can see the difference between the two most popular **Semi-Automatic Pistols** – the 1911 and the **Glock** in the following images:

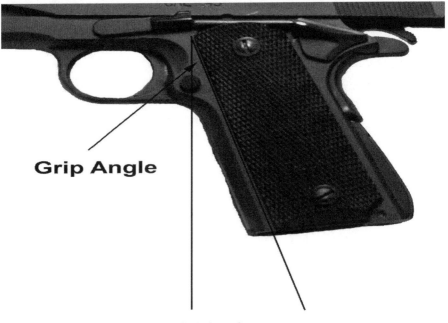

Grip Angle

1911 GRIP ANGLE

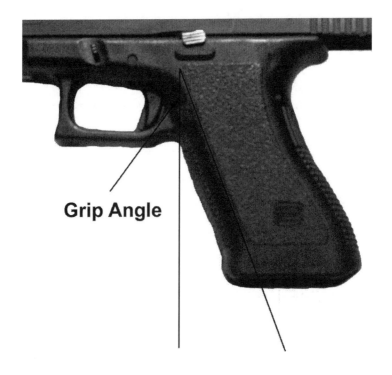

Grip Angle

GLOCK GRIP ANGLE

There have been countless thousands of posts arguing which weapon has the better **Grip Angle** – the **1911** at 11% and the **Glock** at 13%. The purpose of the **Angle** is, again, to channel the recoil down into the shooter's body. The story goes that the **1911** uses the **Angle** of the knuckles of the closed fist of a fighter to find a best fit . The **Glock** uses the same **Angle** but takes it from the striking **Angle** of a martial artist's fist delivering a straight blow. Good stories, logical – but I have no idea if they are true. What IS true is that if, when you wrap either weapon with your dominant hand, you find that it just doesn't feel right – you will likely not shoot well with it.

So, size of the **Grip** – depth and width, the length of the **Grip**, the **Grip Angle**, all contribute to the fit of the weapon feeling natural in your hand.

The grip should be consistent.

Every time you grip your weapon – it should be the same. This allows you to work on your sight picture and not worry if you are holding your weapon effectively for each and every shot. Let's look at what I consider a proper **Grip** for both a revolver and a semi-automatic pistol.

Revolver Grip

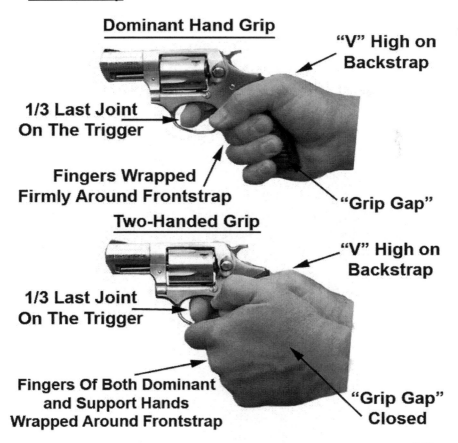

Dominant Hand Grip

"V" High on Backstrap

1/3 Last Joint On The Trigger

Fingers Wrapped Firmly Around Frontstrap

"Grip Gap"

Two-Handed Grip

"V" High on Backstrap

1/3 Last Joint On The Trigger

Fingers Of Both Dominant and Support Hands Wrapped Around Frontstrap

"Grip Gap" Closed

Your **Dominant Hand's** V should be high on the back strap, with the bottom three fingers firmly wrapped around the front strap. You must train your body that your trigger finger is **NOT PART OF THE GRIP!** It has one, and **ONLY ONE** purpose, to press the trigger.

Notice that when you grip your weapon with your **Dominant Hand** only – you leave a **Grip Gap** between your finger tips and the large palm-pad beneath your thumb. When you fire your weapon, the recoil will escape through the area of least resistance, the **Grip Gap**, forcing your weapon to not only recoil rear-ward and down your arm, but also to the right (for right-handed shooters) because the recoil escapes to the left, out your **Grip Gap**. This is simply something to be noted if you are shooting **Dominant Hand** only, because you will have to compensate for it on your follow-up shots. However, if you are using a **Two-Handed Grip**, you can mitigate this problem .

First, take your **Support Hand's** large palm-pad and place it firmly into the **Grip Gap**. Then, wrap your fingers firmly around your **Dominant Hand's** fingers that are already wrapped around the front strap. Place your **Support Hand's** thumb on top of your **Dominant Hand's** thumb. Both hands should then settle into a firm grip – not a death grip. You are trying to control the recoil of the weapon, not choke it to death.

One side note – **DO NOT LET YOUR INDEX FINGER OF THE SUPPORT HAND SPAN THE GAP BETWEEN THE FRONT OF THE CYLINDER AND THE FRAME!** When your cartridge fires, part of the super-heated gasses that are generated escape through this gap and will burn the extended finger. Emulate the grip in the image, and all will be well.

Semi-Automatic Pistol Grip

Notice that virtually all the components of the **grip** are identical to that of the revolver, for exactly the same reasons, with the exception of the thumb on the **Support Hand**. I like to extend it forward along the frame to provide additional purchase on the weapon. And, one additional thing, you do not need to worry about escaping gasses burning your hand as in the revolver; all gasses are contained and either go down the barrel or are captured and used to eject the spent casing and strip a new cartridge off the top of the magazine.

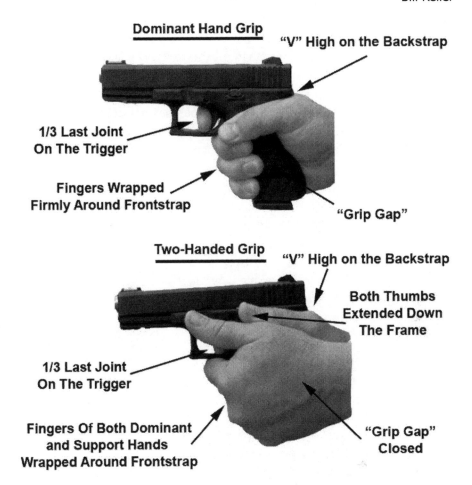

Dominant Hand Grip

"V" High on the Backstrap

1/3 Last Joint On The Trigger

Fingers Wrapped Firmly Around Frontstrap

"Grip Gap"

Two-Handed Grip

"V" High on the Backstrap

Both Thumbs Extended Down The Frame

1/3 Last Joint On The Trigger

Fingers Of Both Dominant and Support Hands Wrapped Around Frontstrap

"Grip Gap" Closed

Make sure your dominant thumb is NOT resting on the slide lock lever, as you may inadvertently lock the slide to the rear during firing.

Your <u>Grip</u> should be firm.

As I said above, your <u>Grip</u> should be firm. You are trying to channel the recoil and aim your weapon, not choke it to death.

I've noticed with new shooters that it is relatively simple to have them using a proper <u>Grip</u> with a .22 <u>Semi-Automatic Pistol</u> pretty quickly. However, when they move up to a <u>**9mm or .40 cal or .45 cal,**</u> all of a sudden their fear of the recoil has them putting their weapon in a death grip. The reality is that simply holding onto the weapon is the least important part of the <u>Grip</u>. It is the channeling of the recoil that is the true purpose of the <u>Grip</u> – to get your mass behind the weapon, to allow your body to absorb the recoil so you can quickly settle your sight picture after a shot and then re-engage your threat. Gripping your weapon harder and harder until your hands tremble does nothing to increase your accuracy or the speed with which you can reacquire your threat.

One brief comment about **Glocks** specifically. Since they are, in large part, polymer – they weigh less than a full sized 1911. However, they still need to capture as much of the energy of the fired cartridge to properly eject the spent casing and to strip a new round off the top of the magazine and fully seat it in the chamber for the next shot. It is not uncommon for new shooters to experience an excessive number of malfunctions involving stove pipes or failures to fully come back into battery (the slide fully forward and the cartridge firmly seated in the chamber). If you are experiencing this, try stiffening your **Dominant Hand's** arm a bit. What's happening is that you are allowing your arm to cushion the recoil. This absorbs some the of recoil energy of the cartridge and rather than being used to cycle the weapon, it moves your arm. This results in the weapon's not having enough energy to fully eject the spent casing or to fully push the slide all the way to the rear so it has enough energy to fully seat the new round.

Stiffen your **Dominant Arm**, lean into the weapon a bit more aggressively, maintain a firm **Grip** and all with be well with the world.

So there you go – if your **Grip** is natural, consistent and firm – you will be able to engage targets or threats quickly and accurately time after time.

The Draw

There is certainly no drought of hot topics to pick on in the *Just the Basics*. And, **the Draw** certainly gets its fair share of attention. So let's talk a bit about **the Draw** – beginning with **the Stance**.

I teach what I call a **Modified-Weaver Stance**;

- Feet shoulder width apart.

- Front toe of your **Dominant Side** even with the heel of your **Support Side**.

- Knees slightly bent.

- Firm, two-handed grip – arms fully extended – body slightly forward in an aggressive position.

There's nothing tricky here, just a nice, stable platform to allow you to engage your threat accurately. This exact **Stance** easily adapts to a rifle or shotgun as well. It allows you to find a single home for your **Stance** that works well with multiple weapons platforms.

This position is also, for most defensive pistol situations, pure crap. Now, why do I say that? Honestly, if you have enough time to put these elements in place for a nice, consistent, well-rehearsed **Stance** – either you should already have left the scene, should long since have engaged the threat – or you are already dead and simply waiting for the bag man.

I have long preached the Rule of Threes with gunfights:

- Three Rounds

- Three Seconds

- Three Meters

Your time is just so compressed. A gunfight isn't going to be pretty, your **Stance** won't be perfect – yet to save yourself, you need to be the first to get off the first of three rounds, make a couple of critical hits and be ready should follow-up shots be required.

So, that means I should abandon any type of* Stance *altogether – right?

No, not at all. I teach this **Stance** and I'll continue to teach it. It's a good

127

starting point. It provides a very stable platform, can be used with other weapons and allows the student to begin to learn the fundamentals of grip, sight alignment, sight picture and trigger press and controlling the weapon in their hand. I simply want a new shooter to be aware that this is an optimal shooting position – not a typical one in an actual fire fight.

There are just a ton of by the numbers draws out there in the shooting universe, from four steps to seven steps or more. I have a different take on it – a task oriented approach. These tasks must be accomplished between the time your mind tells you to DRAW and the time you press off that first round. In general, you must:

- Clear the crap away from the holster

- Grip your weapon

- Withdraw it from its holster

- Point it at the threat and press the trigger

How you accomplish these things are of little importance. That you point and press quickly and accurately – well, that's the difference between a human-sized Ziploc and hugging your kids at the end of the day. For our purposes here, I am just going to go through **the Draw** from concealment as we talk about these different tasks in more detail. If you are in a state with **Open Carry**, and you are – indeed – carrying openly, cover garments will have no part in the equation at all; just skip over the "clear the crap away from the holster" process.

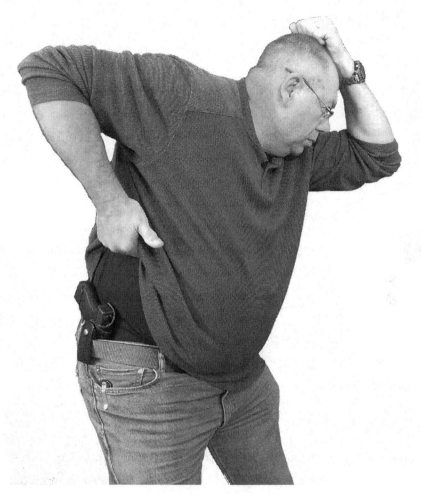

Clear the Crap Away From the Holster.

Again - reality vs. ideal.

Most shooting schools and competitive pistol sports grant you the luxury of sweeping your garment back or sliding your palm and fingers along your body to push your garment back or some such thing. Fine for most cases, especially in competition or on the range – yet what if it's January, -20F, you have a leather coat over a sweater over your holster and gun. Then what? It just got more complicated than sweeping the garment away.

My preferred alternative is **Grasp and Clear.** You grasp the single garment or pile of garments under their hem(s) with the fingers on your **Dominant Hand** and yank them up, well clear of your weapon. Leave your thumb out and above the outer garment. Once you have lifted ALL garments well above the grip of your weapon, you lock them in place by jamming your thumb into your side.

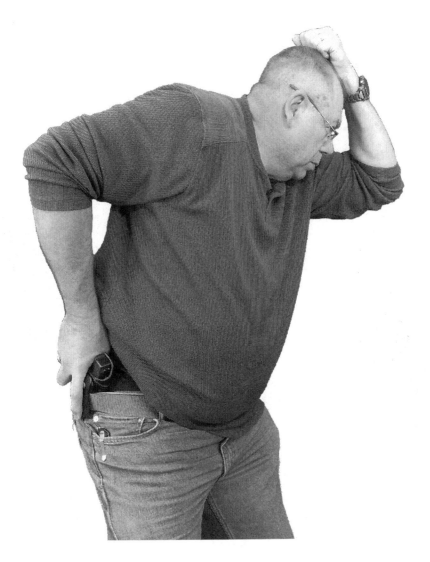

Grip Your Weapon

You then fully extend your fingers. Firmly push the V of your hand (the area between your thumb and index finger) down onto your **Grip**. Your thumb will slide down along your body and go under your **Grip**. Your fingers will go over your **Grip** and wrap around the front strap of the **Grip**. **YOUR TRIGGER FINGER IS NEVER PART OF YOUR GRIP – EVER.** At this point you have a firm grip, your trigger finger is well away from the trigger, and all layers of clothing are trapped between your forearm and your body.

Draw it from the holster

You then draw your weapon straight up until it fully clears your holster. Please note the trigger finger is not just outside the trigger guard – it is on the side of the slide. This digit, this little piece of bone and flesh, is what makes your weapon go BLAM! **Keep the damn thing away from the trigger**.

Point it at the threat and press the trigger

Once the weapon is clear of the holster you begin to rotate it. Once rotated – you are ready to engage. What? What was that?

(**A side note here:** For those weapons with slide safeties – say a __1911__, **THIS** is when the safety comes off. **NOT** during the draw, **NOT** after it clears the holster, **NOT** as it begins to rotate, but **ONLY AFTER IT IS POINTED AT THE THREAT!**)

Yep, you heard me – you are ready to engage. Notice a couple of things in this image. First, my **Support Hand** is up, covering my support side, my face, my head. I have a real problem with teaching shooters to make a fist and place it in the middle of their chest. What the hell for? Is the guy going to punch me there? Will it stop a bullet? I know the argument that you want to make sure it is well out of the way so you don't shoot yourself. Yet, is this truly the muscle memory you want when an attacker comes at you and you need to fend him off while drawing? I don't believe so. Get your **Support Arm** up, out of the way of **the Draw** and into a position to defend your head and face.

Focus on the threat and his center mass. That is your target, that is where you want to hit first – and you want to do that quickly. When your weapon is horizontal, and you are focused on this center mass – shoot him! The numbers say your attacker will be close. The numbers say the first to hit wins the fight. **YOU DO NOT NEED TO BE FULLY EXTENDED IN A TWO-HANDED GRIP TO SHOOT THE BASTARD!**

A solid hit or two will buy you time, force the attacker away and allow you to go into a fully extended shooting **Stance** if need be. Continue to engage the threat the whole time you're extending into a **Two-Handed Grip**. More hits – less of a threat, as simple as that. But, if you wait to engage until you are here – in a full shooting **Stance** – you have lost valuable time and . . . perhaps . . . your life as well.

Once the threat is down keep your distance. Should he attempt to re-engage with his weapon, shoot him. Period. A threat with a weapon in his hand is a threat to your existence – treat him that way.

Once the threat has been neutralized – do not reholster immediately. If you are safe, near cover, assured that there are no other bad guys around – do a tactical reload. Drop your magazine and insert a fresh one, then stow the dropped magazine. This prepares you for the next engagement if necessary.

Call police – or wait for their arrival while keeping your weapon on the threat. Make sure you describe yourself fully to the police prior to their arrival or you could end up on the wrong end of a friendly fire incident. When they arrive, lay your weapon down and put your hands behind your head. **FOLLOW ALL DIRECTIONS.**

You will be arrested, taken to jail, informed of your rights – and your very first call should be to your attorney. Your only comment? "I thought I was going to die!"

That's quite a journey – from **Holster Draw** to jail. Yet, it reinforces the seriousness of drawing your weapon. It should never leave your holster unless you truly believe your very existence is at risk. And, if you feel that way, if a threat is coming at you intent on ending your life – be the one to walk away ... period!

You can do 95% of the training required to learn this **Draw** as part of your dry fire exercise each and every day. Use this method every time you take your weapon from your holster – whether to remove your weapon at the end of the day or to remove it from its holster to take a latrine break. Every time you draw from your holster, it's a training experience.

Ideally your **Draw** is simply a command your brain gives. Everything else is muscle memory. It is one of many steps required to save your life, your family's lives or your friend's lives should you encounter an existential threat. Learn it – practice it – use it ... and then hope that day never – ever comes.

A few words about those elastic cords that seem to be buried in virtually every jacket or heavy coat made today. One of their features is an adjustment to these cords so the fit can be tightened against the cold and wind. In general, they look a bit like this.

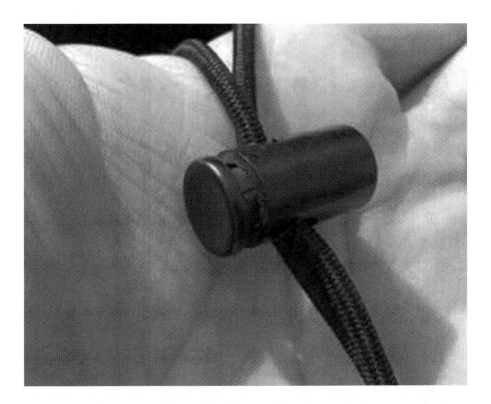

ADJUSTER CORD

These little guys can do real damage to you. There have been any number of reports of them becoming lodged inside the trigger guard and wedging themselves in such a way to depress the trigger and fire off a round as the weapon is either being drawn or reholstered. Cut all such devices off and completely remove the elastic cord. This small step could save you from a very bad day!

Hands, hands ... what the heck do I do with my hands?

A couple of my friends gave me a call about my arm position in the photos of **the Draw**. One of them, a retired Naval Flight Officer – Old NFO – asked me: Why is your **Support Arm** so high and far away from your body?

Phone rings: Keller!

Deep Texas Twang: Bill? It's me, xxxxx, you know Old NFO! *(Have you ever noticed that ALL PILOTS talk like Chuck Yeager?)*

A nice half-hour conversation ensued regarding the position of my **Support Arm** in the photo, what he had been taught, what my reasons were. A very pleasant and informative half-hour at that.

So on to the topic at hand – hands, hands … what the heck do I do with my hands?

Perhaps it should be obvious, but just to cover the most basic element of **Support Hand/Arm position** – KEEP YOU DAMN HAND/ARM AWAY FROM THE MUZZLE OF YOUR WEAPON! Second – these are simply my opinions – other instructors, for other types of training, will have their thoughts, ideas and expectations. Listen to them! Over time you will find your own base set of physical mechanics that fit your body, your way of moving, your level of training. The majority of my students are new shooters, unfamiliar with weapons or personal defense, so I have chosen three positions I encourage them to explore and begin with, to give them a very basic set of defensive positions for their **Support Arm**.

These would be: **Close Chest**, **Forearm Vertical** and **Upper Arm Extended**.

Close Chest: This is the position the NRA teaches for **Dominant Arm** shooting only. Your **Support Arm's** fist is clenched and placed center chest. This provides you, the shooter, the ability to stiffen your upper body and provide greater support for your extended **Dominant Arm** as you shoot. And, it keeps your **Support Hand** well away from your weapon's muzzle.

Forearm Vertical: You, the shooter, take the **Forearm** of your **Support Arm** and place it close to your body in a vertical/horizontal/slanted position to block your attacker. Both the **Close Chest** and **Forearm Vertical** positions provide you good protection and keep your arm close to the body so that it stands less of a chance to become something the attacker can grab and use to his advantage.

Upper Arm Extended: Bend your **Support Arm** at a 90 degree angle and hold your **Support Arm** horizontal in front of you. This distance, the distance your **Upper Arm** is **Extended**, provides you maximum retention of your **Support Arm**. It gives you a great deal of flexibility to block your attacker, while not providing him the ability to grab your arm and push/shove you off balance. Once you begin to extend your **Support Arm**, you provide your attacker an open invitation to simply reach, grab and pull.

Remember, an attack will likely be within 3 yards, last less than 3 seconds and require you to defend yourself with your **Support Arm** while you draw and engage your threat with 3 rounds or less. While there is certainly nothing wrong with working on your fully extended, two handed, solid sight alignment, good sight picture shooting, please - remember - this is an IDEAL situation and one you are not likely to experience.

Gun fights are quick, personal, violent – and at close quarters.

Train that way, learn to defend your off side to gain much needed time to draw and engage your attacker . . .

You may well get but a single chance . . . .

Your Dominant Eye

Dominant: *commanding, controlling, or prevailing over all others*

Our bodies work out a lot of the mechanics of everyday living as we grow. Balance, movement, reaching, the incorporation of vision and touch … it's an amazingly complex machine. It takes years to train.

One of the decisions our bodies usually make is whether an individual is right handed or left handed. It's not that one hand or the other is useless … just which one is dominant , which hand do we prefer to use. There are some folks who are truly ambidextrous – they are fully comfortable using either hand interchangeably. Rare, but they are out there.

Typically, our eyes follow our hand preference. If we are right hand dominant, our body prefers to use our right eye first to focus on an object that we may be reaching for. In the shooting sports – **Eye Dominance** plays an important part in sighted fire, those instances when we take full advantage of sight alignment and sight picture prior to pressing the trigger. So what is an easy way to determine which of our eyes is the dominant one?

Start by extending your arms out in front of you and forming a triangle . . . it looks something like this:

Pick a point in the distance and put it at the center of the triangle. I have chosen the face of an early 1900s Waterbury Clock that sits on our mantel. KEEP BOTH EYES OPEN.

Then, slowly move your hands towards your face, keeping both eyes open and slowly making the triangle smaller and smaller until your hands touch your face and you can still see the clock face.

With your hands touching your face, the triangle intact, both eyes open and the clock face clearly visible … close one eye at a time. DO NOT MOVE YOUR HANDS! The eye you close that makes the clock face disappear is your **Dominant Eye**. Try this exercise a couple of times; you'll get the hang of it.

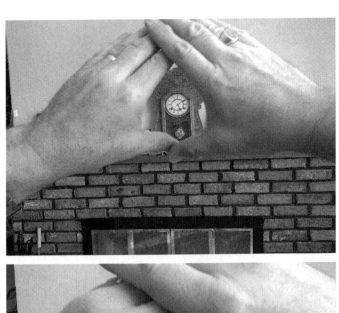

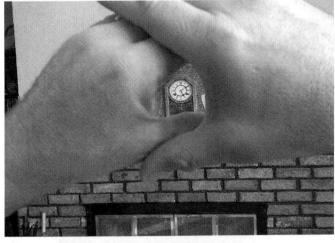

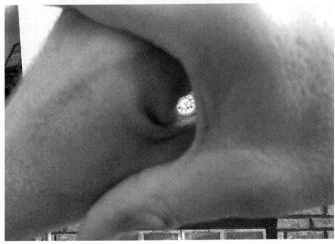

Could you be right handed BUT **left-eye Dominant**? Sure, and just the opposite as well . . . left handed BUT **right-eye Dominant**. This is called **cross-eye Dominant**. For pistol shooting, a small adjustment in your head position can compensate for sighted fire. For defensive fire – metal on meat - **Eye Dominance** has little effect.

However, for long-gun shooting using iron sights or a scope, you may well find it easier to switch shooting hands. Again, **cross-eye Dominant** shooters are not all that common – in the 20% range. And, if you are **cross-eye Dominant**, you can certainly train your body to adapt to either switching shooting hands or using your **Non-Dominant Eye**.

Do this little exercise, figure out which is your **Dominant Eye** and then adapt as necessary.

I Just Can't Hit A Darn Thing With This Thing ...

Firing first shots is always interesting to watch. Having sent more rounds down range over the past 40+ years than I can count, it's easy to forget that first time. Teaching the NRA Basic Pistol course is a nice reminder that while for many of us it's old hat – many folks in our country have never fired a handgun.

I always do a lot of prep work prior to taking the folks out to the range. They practice loading all the firearms I bring with plastic rounds. Single and Double Action Revolvers, .22, 9MM and .45 ACP Semi-Automatic Pistols, Single Stack and Dual-Stack Magazines. All of them. Multiple times.

Then we walk through their stance – I use what I term a modified Weaver – dominant leg's toe even with the heel of the support side, feet shoulder width apart. Knees slightly bent. Shooter leans slightly forward into the firearm using a two-handed grip.

We discover each person's dominant eye (actually had two cross-dominant shooters this last class). Then we work on grip – dominant hand high on the grip, grip well into the V , trigger finger lying on the top of the barrel, support hand palm firmly planted in the gap, fingers wrapped over the dominant hand, thumb pointed down the barrel/slide. A firm grip, not a death grip . Aggressive stance, slightly forward.

We do all this in the classroom. Then we dry fire – work on trigger press. This is followed by an in-depth discussion of sight alignment, sight picture and how this allows them to aim their firearm. I try to work in a wall drill or two to have them watch movement/anticipation as they press the trigger.

Finally, after lunch, (I want them well hydrated and not hungry), we hit the range.

I do first shots with one round only in the magazine. I do that because I have no idea how they will react when their firearm goes BLAM! I want to watch them first.

Once that's done they have 10 rounds of practice on the first target I give them: 10 rounds, 21 feet, slow fire. 99% of the time this is a piece of cake – but every once in a while I have a new shooter who finishes the 10 rounds and has only 1 or 2 hits on the paper. This is usually followed by an embarrassed grumble that sounds something like:

I just can't hit a darn thing with this gun …

I had just such a shooter this past class.

There's a lot working on the mind of a new shooter in his first class. Many are a bit apprehensive, some are frightened, some are only there because their mate/friend pushed them into coming. Most don't want to look stupid in front of strangers – and not hitting the target only amplifies this fear. It's the instructor's purpose to keep them safe, reduce their fears and teach the skillset that will allow them to hit the paper. This is usually the point, with a target that's empty of holes, at which I have everyone just relax, take a deep breath, and go over taking aim with their handgun one more time. I do this at the loading tables as they get ready to reshoot their practice targets. Everyone reshoots, not just the shooter who needs an extra hand. And, it sounds something like this …

Aiming – Sight Alignment, Sight Picture – the elements of Aiming your firearm.

Sight Alignment

This is the skill of properly **<u>Aligning</u>** the **<u>Rear and Front Sights</u>** so that the round you fire hits your expected target. There are all kinds of **<u>Sight Sets</u>** available for handguns, rifles and shotguns. For our purposes we are going to show a simple **<u>Notch and Blade Sight System</u>** and discuss their use for a handgun – though the mechanics remain unchanged for a rifle or shotgun with rifle sights.

A proper **Sight Alignment** looks like this:

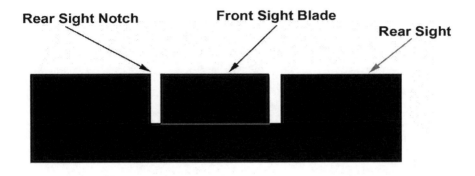

Rear Sight Notch   **Front Sight Blade**   **Rear Sight**

The **Rear Sight Notch** is usually mounted at the rear of the handgun. It is a simple block of metal with a notch milled out of the exact center. It is slightly wider than the width of the **Front Sight Blade**, which is usually mounted on the very front of the firearm, just rear of the muzzle. Above you see what proper **Sight Alignment** looks like – the **Front Sight Blade's** top edge is exactly level with the **Rear Sight's** top edge. The **Front Sight Blade** is exactly in the center of the **Rear Sight Notch** (an equal amount of light is seen on both sides of the **Blade**).

Since both the **Front Sight Blade** and the **Rear Sight Notch** are exactly centered on the centerline of the barrel, you can be assured that when you **Aim** your handgun in this manner, your firearm with strike the target in the intended spot. This process is what is involved when you **Aim** your firearm.

A couple other items come into play as well. It is physically impossible for your eye to focus on the **Rear Sight Notch**, the **Front Sight Blade** and the **Target** at the same time. The physics of the lens in your eye will simply not allow this to happen. Yet, you still need a point of focus. For aimed fire, the **Front Sight Blade** becomes your point of focus. With the **Blade** in focus, the rear **Notch** will be slightly blurry but clear enough to gage equal light on either side of the **Blade** in the **Notch**. The target will be blurry as well, but clear enough to you to properly place your aligned sights on the target, forming the **Sight Picture**.

Sight Picture

There are two common **Sight Pictures** that are seen when you **Aim** your firearm …

Point of Aim

The top of the **Front Sight Blade**, centered in the center of the **Rear Sight Notch**, is centered on the bull's-eye of your target. You **Sight Picture** looks like this. This is a factory setting – or if you have adjustable rear sights – a shooter setting.

There is a second **Sight Picture** that can be seen in firearms when you **Aim** them …

The Lollipop

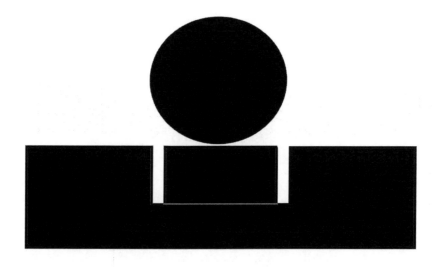

Here the top of the **Front Sight Blade**, which is centered in the **Rear Sight Notch**, is placed just below the bull's-eye of your target. Again, this is either a factory or shooter setting for this particular firearm.

So, if you acquire a good **Sight Alignment**, see a proper **Sight Picture** for your firearm, you're going to hit your target – plain and simple. Anything else – any miss – is all shooter. And there are dozens of little things involved in grip, stance, trigger press that can affect your hit placement. It takes time, persistence, attention to the smallest detail – to resolve these things. But, once you feel what it's like to get solid hits, it gets much easier.

So, back to the class and the new shooter with only three hits or so. Everyone reshoots – it keeps their discomfort down (and can new shooters really shoot too much ?). This time, with focus on **Sight Alignment** and **Sight Picture** – all 10 rounds are on the paper. The beginnings of a new skill are learned – and the qualification target for this shooter, the one I keep for my records, has all 10 rounds within the 8 outer circle of the qualification target. Not bad for her first 31 rounds ever fired.

But, but, but – wait … . . .

Aren't you always harping on this being an entry point for defensive shooting for personal protection? How the heck do I have time to take such careful **Aim** if some bad guy is coming at me?

Good question!

For personal defense, the standard for training has become 21 feet. **This comes from a study that showed the average bad guy could cover 21 feet in 2 seconds** – hence the training distance of 21 feet and the t draw and engage goal. Honestly, there's plenty of meat here for a whole other post. However, I do want to chat quickly about the quality of the **Sight Picture** for a threat that's at 21 feet or less.

At those distances, perfect alignment is simply not needed. If you can see the **Blade** in the rear **Notch**, you will put rounds on target. The **Sight Alignment** looks something like this …

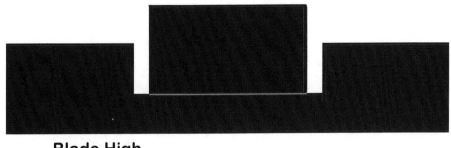

Blade High

Blade Low

Blade Left

Blade Right

If you are **Blade High**, you will hit above the center of the target, but on an 8 x 11 piece of paper at 21 feet if you are **Blade Low**, you will hit below center, but on the paper. **Blade Left** will be left of center and **Blade Right** will be right of center – but both will be on the paper. This drastically reduces the acquisition time for your target. Just see the **Blade** in the **Notch** – and you will get a hit!

So … really … with a little work, an understanding of **Sight Alignment**, **Sight Picture** and a willingness to invest the range time to commit this to muscle memory …

You can hit any darn thing you want!

Metal on Meat

Perhaps one of the greatest frustrations of a new shooter is simply hitting the target, that silly little piece of paper with the black dot and surrounding circles. I have discussed the entire process of stance, grip, sight picture and sight alignment a number of different ways. It should be simple … it doesn't seem to be … even for some old heads .

For many shooters, their range trip consists of standing in a bay, behind a bench, with their weapon, ammunition and magazines in front of them. Their time is spent making holes in paper with the intent of having the smallest grouping possible. There's nothing wrong with this at all. It's a good way for a new shooter to learn the basics of stance, grip, sight alignment, sight picture, trigger press … and getting familiar with their weapon. This is all good stuff! However, it is also very limiting and can introduce some habits that could prove fatal in a defensive situation.

Remember, most defensive shootings follow the Rule of Three – 3-rounds, 3-yards, 3-seconds. From the identification of a threat until the end of the engagement … 3 seconds. Obviously, if you take the time to draw, get a nice stance and firm grip, align your sights so you are aimed center mass of your threat … you may well go home in a Ziploc. You do not have time for the fine points. And, you have no need for them.

What is working both against you – and for you – is the distance to the threat. You don't need to get fancy, you simply need to place **Metal on Meat** to get combat effective hits. These are hits on the threat that do damage, cause pain and are used to either change his mind about his attack on you … or to put him down.

What the heck does **Metal on Meat** look like? Well, it looks something like this:

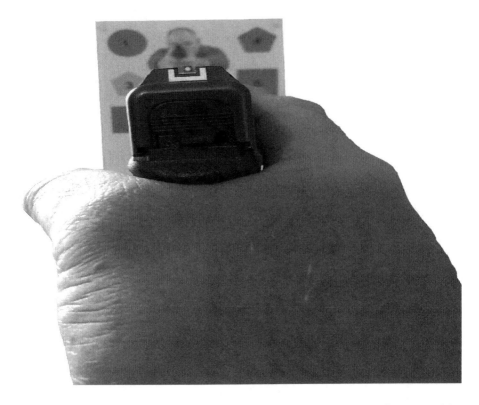

You're looking at a 1/3 sized IDPA target at an equivalent distance of 21 feet (those three above are ¼ sized and are used to simulate a threat 30 feet away). The weapon in my hand is my new **SIRT Pistol** from **NextLevel Training**. It has the form factor of a **Glock 17**. Notice that the **Metal** (the rear of the slide) is completely covering the **Meat** of the target – center mass of an oncoming threat at 21 feet. For the training I do – this is about the furthest distance for this type of shooting. You take one or two hands, grip the weapon, place your **Metal** on their **Meat** and press the trigger 2-5 times. No worries about stance, sight alignment, sight picture – just cover them with the back of your weapon and shoot.

A good way to introduce yourself to this type of shooting is to purchase a LaserLyte round for your weapon, print out a 1/3 sized IDPA target, tape it to a safe wall, insert your LaserLyte round in your weapon and practice your draw stroke and first-round hit. Change your focus to the threat … draw your weapon … join and extend … and as SOON AS YOU HAVE **METAL ON MEAT** , press the trigger. Begin slowly, work through the process and then gradually work up your speed with a sub-two second goal for your first hit.

Once you are satisfied with this for dry fire, practice it on the range. Start slowly … no need to add holes to your body! If you can't draw at your range, work from the low ready. Keep both your eyes open. Focus on the threat. Work at distances from 21 feet to 9 feet. I suspect you will be surprised how quickly this skill can be learned.

Time is life – it's as simple as that. Spend too much time getting your aim right … your day will not end well. **Metal on Meat** is one of the building blocks of defensive shooting. It's quick, it's accurate enough for the task at hand … and it needs to be part of your skill set.

Sights … sights … which one is the BEST?

So I'm at the range just checking things over before I head home for the evening. I'm an RSO there and everyone once-in-a-while our shooters are not very good at housekeeping, so I stop by frequently for a look-see . A fellow is there with his son and one of his son's friends sighting in his new .308 black gun on the 50 yard range. He's hitting slightly above the target stand and 2 feet to the left … it's not going well. (Discussions days later revealed the previous owner knew little about a proper scope mount and after realignment of the scope's centerline and a bit of Loc-Tight, things came around.) Anyway, the boys and I start discussing an upcoming rifle shoot I'm putting together for the chapter in September. We have a 100 yard range only – so we will use the NRA reduced targets. It's not a sanctioned shoot – just for fun and bragging rights.

"So what kind of scope do you use, Bill?" The shooter's son is pretty darn impressed with the hardware sticking up from the upper of his dad's latest purchase.

Actually, I don't use a scope and the shoot will be **Iron Sights** only.

This is met with an incredulous look by the boy and his dad. "Really?" goes the chorus of replies.

"Yep, really. I typically don't use scopes." There's still a puzzled look on both of their faces. Really? No scope?

So let's chat a bit about **Sights** – and which ones are BEST. (You thought discussions about the best holster could run long … .)

First off – there are **NO BEST Sights** – but there are solid approaches to choosing **Sights** for your intended use of the weapon.

I teach my courses from a personal defense POV. I'm not into tacticool, I'm not a sniper looking to drop an intruder at 600 yards and I'm not an extreme hunter looking for that 800 yard long-distance kill. I focus on the up-close and personal gunfight – from body-to-body contact out to maybe 50 feet. After that – if you're hosing the area around a threat past 50 feet – things will not go well for you in court. If I do need to reach out and touch someone, 100 yards – in a personal defense environment – is more than enough – IMNSHO, of course. So, most encounters will be of the **Metal**

on Meat variety, not precision fire. Most will demand rapid acquisition, not small group precision. This brings me back to the primary type of **Sight** that comes on virtually all defensive weapons – pistol, rifle, shotgun – the **Iron Sight**.

Given that limitation, there are still countless **Iron Sights Pairs** available on the market today. So let's look at a few different kinds, what they offer the shooter and see where they fit in the scheme of things. Since I have a fondness for **Glocks**, I'll start there.

These are simple **Sights** that are standard on a **Glock**. They are **Fixed Sights**, meaning that actual adjustments are made with a specific **Glock** rear-sight adjustment tool and a file for the front post. Which implies that you should let a certified **Glock** armorer do this task if need be.

On the left is a simple **3-Dot Sight System**. Indentations on either side of the **Rear Sight Notch** that are filled with a white paint – same with the **Front Post**. When the dots are straight across – you have proper **Sight Alignment**. The white dots are more visible in standard light – but darkness diminishes your ability to acquire a **Sight Picture**.

Enter the center choice and a **Tritium Sight**. These white dots gather energy from light and then glow in the dark, providing you much greater ability to acquire a **Sight Picture** in low light.

Finally, the outlined **Notch** on the **Rear Sight** and white dot on the **Front Blade**. Put the ball in the basket and you are on-target. This is my favorite and is on my **Glock** carry weapon. However, they are NOT glow in the dark.

These are basic **Sights**; they require no extras (batteries, more holster space, special weapon mounts). They will be available and functional each and every time you draw your weapon.

There are a multitude of alternatives on this particular variation – above are some examples. My son likes the **TruGlo** option on his IDPA weapon and it has made a real difference for him. The bottom line is that these types of **Sighting Systems** are self-contained and require no special mounts or power. I Being in a place where FUBAR (F*#@ed) Up Beyond All Repair) is operating in all its glory is a very bad place indeed. And, when you are dependent on that system for personal defense – the fewer parts to break or run out of energy, the better. Simple **Iron Sights** are my personal choice and what I strongly encourage my students to get very familiar with and to use on their defensive weapons.

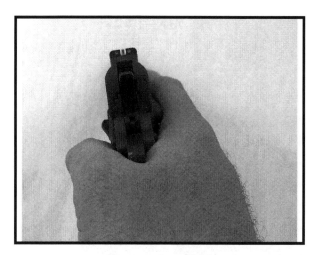

SPRINGFIELD 1911

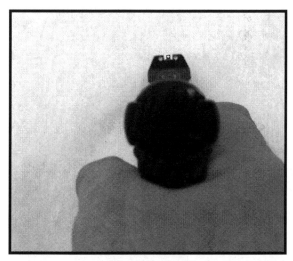

RUGER SIGHTS

SEMI-AUTO SIGHTS

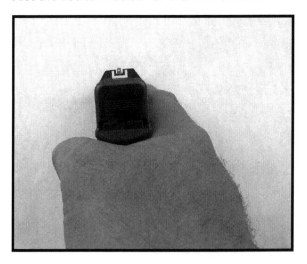

GLOCK SIGHTS

That said – there some alternative options that offer benefits that are certainly worth a look. For my long gun I have a **Panther Arms AP4** in 7.62. I have removed the carry handle, installed a pop-up **Rear Sight** as well as an **EOTECH Holographic Sight**.

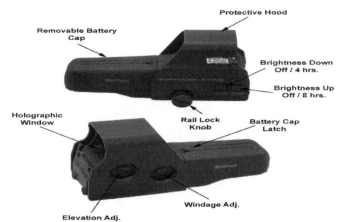

EOTech 517 Holographic Weapons Sight

This, to me, is the best of both worlds. The **EOTECH** provides very quick target acquisition (anything with a red dot on it will have a very bad day) with broad situational awareness (you can easily keep both eyes open and the red dot on the primary threat). Yes, it runs on batteries, yes you need to have spares in the stock or your kit. But, the trade-off is solid to me.

One caution with a **Holographic Sight**, there is a very strong temptation to align the red dot with the top of your **Front Sight**. Avoid this temptation – put the red dot on the target and ignore your **Front Post**. And, if you are using your **Front and Rear Iron Sights** – ignore the red dot . They are typically NOT usable together.

And – if your batteries fail – the **Rear Sight** sits at the right height to allow you to see through the **EOTEC Sight** and use the **Front Post** normally. This combination meets all my requirements of a solid and flexible **Aiming System** for my long gun within the 100 yard range.

A popular alternative **sighting System** for handguns is a **Laser System** of some type. The big dog in that market is **Crimson Trace**. They offer a variety of mounting systems including some that simply require a **Grip** change to be ready to go.

CRIMSON TRACE LASER SYSTEM

There are obvious advantages to this type of system – put the laser dot on the threat, a bad day for them will quickly follow. And, obviously the shooter will always have the **Primary Sights** on the weapon for backup. So, as with the **EOTECH on AP4**, this offers both options. The only thing I have noticed with folks using this type of system is that they quickly become dependent on it and all work with the old **Iron Sights** quickly stops. I believe this to be a mistake. And I believe it strongly enough that I suggest folks put off such a **Sighting System** until they are full proficient with good old **Iron Sights**.

One other thing to remember: if your **Grips** are changed to include a **Laser Sight** or different **Rear Sight** and **Front Blade**, make sure they will still fit your carry holster. It can be a bit of a surprise if you suddenly you get your weapon back from the armorer and it simply no longer fits your holster.

One final option for your defensive carry pistol is a **Slide Mounted Optic**. If you are looking at these my only response is … . really?

So there ya go, a quick spin through a bunch of different **Sighting Systems**. Your needs may differ, your defensive approach may vary from mine. Spend some time thinking about your use, trying different systems and then pick one that you can use to quickly and consistently get on target to stop whatever threat is headed your way.

Pull the damn trigger!

I'm around nine or ten and Uncle Ted is standing behind me, shirtless, smokin', hands on his hips, waiting for me to pull the damn trigger on the .22 Colt Woodsman I am shooting for the first time. We are at his cabin up north in Michigan and I am getting my first shooting lessons. (Just goes to show, we are taught bad habits early in life.) For a ten year old, the Colt Woodsman is a sizable piece of iron to be holding for the first time. I am being taught old school stance – bladed 45 degrees to the target (a 7-Up can), support hand in my rear pocket, arm full extended, good sight picture and finally, "Pull the damn trigger, Bill!" I still remember how the Colt wavered and shook – I could not hold a sight picture to save my soul. Finally, responding to Uncle Ted's frustrations, as well as my own, I pulled the trigger – and was astounded that the can shot off the stump, a clean little hole in its middle.

Well, Uncle Ted slapped me on the shoulder, laughed and gave me a "Nice shootin'." I was pretty darn proud of myself as well, happy with my performance – with my initial impression of proper stance and trigger pull imprinted on my ten year old mind.

Well past my formative years, my initial pistol training was conducted by Tiny the Taiwanese MP. Nothing changed – bladed stance, support hand in rear pocket, arm extended, fairly solid sight picture (I was considerably stronger by then) and my trigger pull. Let's just say, accuracy was not one of my strong points. Things began to change in the pistol shooting world –

Jeff Cooper began to talk about trigger squeeze – others talked about trigger press. Stances changed with the introduction of the Weaver and Isosceles – increasing stability and accuracy. And – I began to move as well, finding my new position – my new shooting home so to speak. It has settled into what I call a **Modified Weaver** – feet shoulder width apart, dominant side foot toe even with the rear of the support side foot, two-handed grip, arms extended, both eyes open, solid sight picture … . and NO TRIGGER PULL … but a **Trigger Press**.

What's the best way to explain **Trigger Press**? Well, demonstration usually has a tendency to be more descriptive than words, so let me show you how I teach **Trigger Press** to new shooters. I use a simple ball point pen, cradle it in my strong side hand, I use the very end 1/3 of my **Trigger Finger** to gently press the **Trigger**.

The tendency of many new shooters is to incorporate the **Trigger Finger** as one of the parts of the strong side hand that grips your weapon – IT IS NOT! The ONLY PURPOSE of the **Trigger Finger** is to PRESS THE **TRIGGER**! Period. So, spend some time with this training device and see if it improves your accuracy.

FIGHT! – Combat-Effective Shooting

We have chatted about what happens when time runs out – that moment when you draw your weapon to stop the threat that is before you. Now what? Well, the obvious answer is SHOOT THE BASTARD! NOW!

At that instant your body undergoes a massive adrenaline dump – your eyesight drops to about 35 degrees per eye – 70 degrees total. Your fine motor skills are gone and you are left with only your gross motor skills (making constant practice manipulating your weapon a must). Your heart rate sky-rockets, your breathing becomes rapid. All this occurs while an existential threat intending to send you home in a box is bearing down on you.

A number of studies have been conducted regarding the mechanics of gunfights. Perhaps one of the most unique and comprehensive is _Shooting to Live by Fairbairn and Sykes_. Their first-hand experience with approximately 600 gunfights is not only a gripping read but also very informative. Discussions cover distances, types of weapons, body armor, movement – to name just a few topics. If you have not read this book – stop now (I'll wait), go to Amazon and place it on order – you will not be sorry. In today's vernacular, perhaps the most common title assigned to describe their shooting technique would be **Combat Effective Shooting**.

Keeping in mind most gun fights obey a **Rule of Three** – 3 rounds, 3 seconds, 3 meters. Your ability to shoot a threat bears no resemblance to standing on a firing line, carefully taking your stance, your grip, acquiring a good sight alignment and sight picture and engaging the threat. A gun fight is fast, brutal and deadly. In general, the shooter to get the first hit wins. Time spent working on combat-effective hits will serve you well.

When looking at an active threat, you should work on three primary skills:

MOVE – a stationary target is a dead target. I hear the words "get off the x" used frequently, but basically you want to make yourself into a moving target, not a stationary one.

DRAW – work on your draw stroke daily. Dry fire, draw slowly until it's perfect – then accelerate it until you fail, back off a bit and repeat – daily.

POINT AND SHOOT – work on the **Metal on Meat Sight Picture**, put the rear of your weapon in the center of the chest and pull the trigger as fast as you can until the threat is stopped..

The hits you achieve in this three-step process would fit into the category of combat effective shooting; you're not going to have nice, tight 3-inch groups, all your rounds will not be going through the same hole – yet you have the opportunity to significantly damage your immediate threat.

So where should you **Aim**? There are three primary areas and one that spans the three.

First, **Center Chest**. A round of Critical Defense ammunition from

154

Hornady through a threat's heart will be a bad day for any attacker. Multiple rounds in the area of the heart and lungs will go a long way to take your attacker's mind off you and make him stop threatening you.

Next, the **Pelvic Area**. Break the pelvis, the attacker's mobility is severely limited; and it's an area where the majority of your blood supply is generated. You can dump a lot of blood in a short time through multiple pelvic hits.

Third, the head also provides the opportunity to quickly stop the threat, yet it is no guarantee; and trying to hit a four-inch target during an adrenaline dump can require more luck than you have at that given instant.

Finally, the ultimate off switch, the **Spine**. Sever his spine above the pelvis, his legs stop; sever his spine above his heart – his primary systems stop; sever his spine at the throat – he drops like a rock and you are no longer threatened.

I teach a new shooter to focus on the torso, from the neck to the crotch. I have him experience dumping multiple rounds in that region, from a number of different positions, while using various point shooting tools – focus on the target, use your entire weapon to aim - not just the front sight, engage early and often. My goal is 3-5 rounds in this area in less than three seconds. Most threats will be down at the end of this process – not all of them, but most of them. For those still presenting a danger, repeat above as needed.

Bottom line: stop worrying about small groups on little round targets at 21 feet. Death will greet you at a much more intimate distance. Prepare for that moment by ensuring you can get solid **Combat-Effective Hits** quickly and consistently. As I said earlier, you have all the time you need to prepare . . . now. Make use of it.

CHAPTER 6 – TRAINING

TRAINING IS SUCH A BROAD TOPIC. IT CAN COV-
er everything from the training you receive firing your very first
shots to a LEO course that teaches you how to clear a building.
It can be conducted in a rigid, low intensity manner or can be a full-fledged
force-on-force encounter. Under it all is a common goal – to teach you a new
skill set and to provide you the tools you need to hone this new skill set on
your own.

So, do you need training? And if so – what kind?

Training – No, no … that's actually the TITLE of this chapter

Seems to be the current topic lately that's flying around the gun blogs I
read. Train more, train less, train harder, train like you fight, proper form,
proper approach, good trainers, bad trainers … . . . . yeah.

I suppose this chapter is just a bit self-serving because I am – at least in my
mind – a trainer – a person who imparts the knowledge I have, the methods
I use, the approach I like – to students who look over my blog, company site
and reviews and decide to come and spend their time and money with me.
Yep, I am a trainer.

So let me share some of my thoughts with you about training, what to look
for, how to evaluate a trainer and what all this means to you – a new shooter.

Do I need training? Well, it depends on why the heck you bought a gun in the first place. A few examples:

Cool gun to hang over the fireplace? Nope – skip the training.

EVERY OTHER FRICKING PURPOSE UNDER THE DAMN SUN? Why, yes – some training would be advised.

Perhaps a bit finer definition of the word **Training**. Let's go lowest requirement and work our way up and see where that takes us.

I just want to shoot the squirrels that are chewing large honking holes in my house or I just want to kill the armadillos that are ripping the crap outta my back yard. (These are two actual conversations I have had over the past year.) Well, **Training** in this case began with weapon selection (both a nice air rifle with hunting pellets), range time with a target and box in the back yard, confidence in the **4 RULES OF SAFETY** and the general use of the weapon of choice and, voila , the **Training** is complete. Other than on-going target practice (though one got his with a laser sight) they are good for life – spend your money on a night out with the little woman!

Next level – hunting (something other than squirrels and armadillos). OK, **Training** here begins with defining the type of hunting you want to do, the location you want to do it in, the firearm rules of the state and county and then making a weapon selection. Once that is done, I see two paths. Meet the requirement of the state to purchase a license (most require a hunter safety course as a minimum) and then find a good friend to sponsor you in your hunting endeavor. This becomes your **Training** – everything from the right ammunition to how to track, set blinds, handle close/medium/long range shots. And, finally, how to choose your animal, properly harvest it and field dress it as well as store and prepare it. My only golden rule of hunting – you eat what you kill. And yes, that means sparrows, robins or any other stupid choice your child makes with their BB gun during hunting season . THEY WILL ONLY DO IT ONCE!

The thing I notice about hunters is that most of the **Training** evolves into information revolving around the game animal, the habitat selection of a hunt and the stalk itself. Once hunters are comfortable with hitting their target – **Shooting Training** seems to end.

Next up – **Personal Defense**. This is certainly a topic that has exploded over the past couple of years. In fact it was the change in Iowa law – moving from a MAY issue state to a MUST issue state that nudged me to starting e.IA.f.t. So, to answer the basic question – do I need **Training**? If the immediate answer in your head is hell, no – I want you to take a deep breath … I want you to think about your skill set as it exists today … Close your eyes and picture yourself on your last range trip. How was your draw? Were your speed reloads and tactical reloads smooth? What about your time to first round hit … under two seconds? On target? Were 80% or more of your hits combat effective? How's your situational awareness? Are you confident – in your heart of hearts – that should the need arise you could absolutely, without fail, defend yourself – your family – your friends? If there is the slightest doubt, the briefest of hesitation in your thoughts … well then …

Yes, grasshopper – you need **Training**. So what does this mean exactly – **Training**? At the basic level (for simplicity I am going to stick with handguns for this post) the most basic question I get is so, what kind of handgun do I need – I hear **Glocks** are great! Perhaps a little more knowledge is needed prior to weapon selection. For example, can you kill a person? Just a thought. Past that one small item . . .

Do you have any physical limitations, how strong are your hands, how big are they, do you plan to carry, how do you plan to do this . . . and these are just the basic questions. Good, solid **Training Programs** will answer these and more. And, that is the purpose of the **NRA Basic Pistol** and **First Shots Programs**. These **Programs** (or similar **Programs**), will answer most of these questions and put you on a sound footing to move forward. And yes, I know many folks get all pissy about the NRA and their courses – but for a starting point, with instructors who have been trained and evaluated, you could do worse, much worse.

Next step with personal defense – **Carrying Your Weapon**. I've been to a basic course, what more could I possible need other that more range time? As soon as you pass this question – you have entered another phase of **Training**. In the defensive pistol world this moves you to re-evaluate your weapon choice, selection of holsters, belts, magazine carriers, ammunition, secondary weapons – a pretty broad list of knowledge that is greatly facilitated by an instructor.

And, at this level, testosterone begins to be a factor in the instructor community. Everything from combat vet – run and gunners, to grizzled old farts like yours truly – who know everything about everything. Honestly, it's just the way we are – all of us – and if anyone denies that, they're lying. Of course, if an instructor is not confident in his ability to carry a weapon and employ it to protect himself , his family or folks around him, why the hell would you want him as an instructor in the first place?

So, how does selection go forward for you from here? Luckily, in today's world you have your little friend – the Internet. Gunnies talk about everything – instructors, course materials, course videos – everything imaginable. Bottom line, it's YOUR money – read trainer and course evaluations, look up any YouTube videos you can find to see if it's what you're looking for, ask for references, talk to other students – MAKE AN INFORMED DECISION – then tell anyone else who dings you about your course/instructor choice to go to hell – it's your choice.

As for the "Do I need **Training**?" question, just think about the decision you have just made. You have bought a tool that, with the simple press of the trigger, can end a life. You feel uncomfortable enough in your environment that you believe carrying one of these tools 24/7 sounds like a good idea. And, you have made that decision that yes – in an existential threat situation – you could use your tool to kill the attacker. Maybe it's just me – but this choice of tool just screams out for more **Training**. Doesn't it?

So, bottom line, get **Training**, make informed decisions about weapons purchases, find reputable **Trainers** to give you the basics, grow from there. Be satisfied with YOUR choices – demand excellence from your **Trainers**.

Finally – carry your weapon – period. Things go sideways when you least expect it. If your dying thought is damn, should have brought my gun today, should have been able to clear that double feed, wonder why I pulled the trigger and it didn't go bang … .

Shame on you.

Training to the point of failure

System failure is a bitch!

July, 1969 and I'm sitting on a runway at the US airbase at Tainan, Taiwan. I'm being deployed to an island about seventy miles away, off the western coast, called Ma-Gung (seems the world now calls it whatever the Red Chinese wants to call it). My mode of transportation? **A Taiwanese Air Force C-119**. Yep, a no kiddin' Flying Boxcar first made famous by the Berlin Air Lift. It's an odd mix of military protocol and civilian passengers. The pilots give a nice little pre-flight brief, (in Mandarin, of course), the civilians applaud. Then they return forward to the cockpit and we settle into the web seats – military, civilian, commercial air freight, military equipment – all crammed into a nice, tight little hold. It is all very Kurt Vonnegut – Catch 22ish.

The nick name for a C-119 … Flying Brick.

Lead sentence of this chapter … System failure is a bitch!

About half way through the flight – fifteen minutes or so – you hear the kind of bang that takes you to the oh, shit! , think I'm gonna fill my pants, hope I don't scream like a baby place as the aircraft lurches to the right and feels like the high-speed down elevator in Sears Tower.

We have experienced the catastrophic failure of the starboard engine and we ARE going down – Flying Brick, remember. I've been in the Air Force for right at one year, am going to my first TDY duty assignment, have never experienced the joys of FUBAR common in all military environments … and now I am going to die. Well, shit!

Obviously, it was not my day. The pilot did whatever magic he needed to do, and though our decent was constant and steady after the engine failure, we touched down at the very, very, very, very end of the runway and rolled up to a holding point as fire trucks surrounded us and got ready to extinguish a – thankfully – non-existent fire.

The ramp dropped, the pilots emerged to the applause of the passengers and I was off to my new duty assignment – none the worse for wear.

This was my introduction to the dangers of complete and unexpected system failure. I'd love to say it was my last – but twenty-one years in the military assured me that FUBAR was real, prevalent and could make your day a very bad day indeed.

So what the heck does this have to do with personal defense(other than the fact that I enjoy telling tales)? What systems do you, as a shooter and as an individual committed to the defense of yourself, your family and those around you use in a day that could fail and put you in a world of hurt?

Many more than you think. Run your day through in your mind from the time you plant your feet on the floor until you roll back into the sack.

- Electrical grid
- Alarm clock
- Water and Sewer systems
- Your vehicle
- Virtually all municipal systems
- Communication systems – cell, radio, tv, cable
- Public alarm systems – fire, nuclear power plant, intrusion
- Your personal weapons system that you carry in your EDC system
- Your home defense weapons

There are more, but the idea is that in today's world we are, in many ways, dependent on multiple systems that are complex beyond words. They are all subject to failure of one type or another – and each failure, should it happen at a critical moment for you, can make you have a very bad day.

However, behind all of these systems is the most critical system of all – you. Your body is the single most important system that determines your experience of life.

A while back a friend discussed her martial arts training with me and things that were holding her back. Well, after her next trip to the trainer, it was obvious she had hopped right over whatever speed-bump was in her way about fighting and had had her butt handed to her. Honestly, a big step for her, but not without some unintended consequences. Which led to my post on my blog regarding her thread about training limits and techniques and more than a few days of pondering about **Training to Failure** … hence, this chapter.

For the purpose of this chapter, I want to focus on the **Physical Failures** each shooter experiences as he trains for personal defense, some cautions, and some suggestions on how to continue to expand your defensive envelope to make yourself quicker and more lethal.

So, let's chat about … You.

Physical Structure

You are what you are. And with that come the characteristics of the basic machine, whether male or female. Skeletally, you are either short or tall or somewhere in between. You may have physical limitations in your foundation – an imperfect structure, a structure missing components, a damaged structure due to accident or health issues. Yet, this is what you have, this is what you start working with. There is little you can do at this foundational level.

Internal Systems

A quick walk through your innards reveals an amazingly complicated system, well integrated and seriously interdependent. Brain to nerves, nerves to organs, organs providing the nutrients to serve the brain and nerves, muscle, tendons to provide mobility – all controlled by the brain and nerves. Heart and lungs to provide nutrients and oxygen to the brain, nerves and muscles. Damage any system in any significant way – your life will be significantly changed or will end.

Brain

What an interesting system. The easy comparison is to a computer – hardly accurate, at any level. Your brain does manage your major system groups, but it is also home to your personality, your dreams, your desires, your hopes, your fears. It IS you. Damage this system in a significant way – again the outcome will go badly.

You have some control

You have control over various parts of these primary systems. For you entering defensive training, the physical capabilities and the mental conditioning are critical. If you choose to be fat, out of shape, unwilling to eat right, exercise your body, train your muscles – you limit your ability to respond to threats, you limit your ability to be lethal. That's certainly your choice to make. If it's not what you want, choose differently.

If you don't push your mental limits – place yourself in fearful situations, expand your boundaries of risk taking – you also limit your ability to respond to threats and your ability to be lethal. You can use training to first find your limits – then to expand them.

Physically, start with a walk/run and find your limits. Begin training times at 15 minutes (if you're out of shape), 30 minutes if feel like you're in shape.

Pay attention to your heart rate. There are any number of web sites dedicated to helping you find good training zones given your age, weight and general condition. Use them. Then – after a couple of weeks of effort and conditioning – **Train to Failure.** Push yourself at the walk or run until you've simply had it. Back off, use the tools, do the work – then a couple of weeks later **Train to Failure** once again. If you are not **Pushing to Failure** periodically, you are not growing, not becoming as strong as you could, not expanding your limits, not becoming more lethal to those who would wish to do you harm. This should be a lifelong process. While your physical ability can change throughout your life due to illness, accident or simply the characteristics of age – it remains import to **Train to Failure** so you know what your **Failure Points** are. Once you know them, you can adjust your training and equipment to compensate for them. Where do you carry, what do you carry, how wide is your yellow zone, your red zone – if you know your limits, you can adjust to them.

You are an individual system. In order to defend yourself, YOUR system must be battle-ready 24/7. Is this always possible? Nope. I find my body needs to curl up and heal once in a while – as everyone's does. However, when you physically train, especially hand-to-hand, I see little value in training in a way that physically damages you and takes you out of the fight. While that is done and expected in full-on military training, their resources are deep and an injured soldier can be removed from a mission and replaced with a healthy soul. You, however, ARE the army. When YOU are down, your ARMY is down and your DEFENSES are down. Broken arms, legs, fingers, ribs do little to allow you to respond to an intruder or a gunman in the same 7-11 you just walked into. I see little value in this. So, train lighter? No, of course not. However, I do recommend using enough protective equipment to dampen the injuries while still allowing full strength training. Use pads, use head protection. Less macho? Sure, I guess – however, when a goober seeks to do you harm on the way home from the gym or as you are settling in for an evening with the family, you'll be able to respond quicker.

Range Training

Training to Failure is difficult on many ranges. In our area most ranges do not even allow holster draws, let alone shooting while moving, multiple target engagement or switching between multiple weapons systems. Yet, this is what you need to train for. Let's look at the individual components.

Holster Draw

How fast can you get your weapon into the fight from your normal carry position? I DO NOT mean from your favorite holster that you like to train with on the range or in the shooting classes you take. (For me personally, this would be a **Glock 17** in a **Serpa Holster.**) What I mean is drawing from concealment. A substantial portion of your **Draw Stroke** is muscle memory. You brain thinks **Draw** and your weapon appears in front of you, ready to put the threat down. You DO NOT need range time to train your muscles – you need lots of **Draws**, thousands of **Draws** – perfect **Draws**. I would encourage you to set aside fifteen minutes a day to do as many PERFECT **Draws** as you can – each and every day. **Train to Failure** – if your **Draw** fails, fight through it, get on the threat and press the trigger. Once you can do fifteen minutes' worth of **Draws** perfectly – accelerate the **Draw** until you **Fail** – and repeat, EVERY DAY until you get twenty-five perfect draws – then accelerate … … .

Live Fire

Training involves risk. **Weapons Training** involves risk of death – period. Yet, If you never **Train to Failure** during live fire – you do not condition yourself for a full engagement . For this – twenty-five perfect **Draws** per week at the range. I would suggest you back off just a tad from your max dry-fire speed – yet ride that limit as closely as you can.

You are most at risk during the **Draw** and **Reholster**. PAY FRICKING ATTENTION! Muzzle discipline, finger discipline, work the safety, use the safety. There are innumerable **YouTube videos of experts who shoot themselves during quick draw training.** You, too, have the opportunity to appear on international YouTube! You, too, have the opportunity to screw up and put a hole through your leg, foot, arm or other body part. There is risk in everything – that's why you **Train** – to REDUCE your risk – NOT to eliminate it.

Once you are happy with your **Draw**, add movement. AS you **Draw** – MOVE! The five most common directions are: straight at the threat, 2 o'clock, 5 o'clock, 7 o'clock and 10 o'clock. Add this component to your **Dry-fire Exercise** first. Once you are confident, add it to your **Live Fire Training**. Next to actually carrying a weapon each and every hour of each and every day you are awake – learning to move and shoot will do the most to save your life in an actual encounter.

The process is the same – find your limits. Work on a different direction each day during your fifteen minutes of **Dry Fire Practice**. Once you have as many perfect move and **Draw** rounds under your belt as you can get, go faster … repeat.

And, again, once this process is fully learned in a **Dry Fire Mode** –

move it to the range and **Live Fire**. (Note – please, work with your RSO and your range before you do this, or you will quickly find yourself out on your ear with a note to never return.) Movement, rapid **Draw Stroke** and **Combat-Effective Hits** are your goal and will keep you in your family's life rather than in the family plot.

Training, in all things, is the path to learning that skill set. **Training to Failure** allows you to monitor your growth, to see the progress you are making, to refine your technique, to grow. Unless you are pushing your limits – you are stagnant. And, as they say you don't want to be that guy …

Train to Failure … the secret to success.

Three Guns Every New Shooter Should Have In Their Range Bag

One of the questions that people in my shooting classes frequently ask is,"What gun should I buy?" The reality is that when they finish the class they don't know enough to know what kind of gun to purchase. However, I strongly believe there are three guns everybody should have in their range bag, and I'd like to talk about that a little bit.

Each of these guns performs a specific function and their purpose is to build the shooter's shooting skills. The first is a **gas powered air soft**, the second is a **Ruger 22/45** and the final one is a **Glock 17**. Let me talk about each of these and I'll share with you why I think they need to be part of everybody's range bag.

A new shooter is trying to learn a number of new skills and he's trying to learn these skills safely. That, to me, is where the **air soft pistol** comes into play. I recommend a gas powered one so the shooter can shoot more than one round without having to charge the pistol. The normal **gas powered air soft** has a magazine that holds 15 of the 6 mm BBs. And many of them have the same type of form factor as many of the popular handguns so that they'll fit many of the common holsters that are out there. This provides the perfect platform to practice stance, draw from a holster, weapon rotation and joining of the hands, acquiring a sight picture, and finally doing everything from one to three-round engagement with the threat. The nice thing about an **air soft** is that a shooter can practice all day long with little expense, without worrying about weather – especially if he doesn't have access to an indoor range. He can grab much more practice time by setting up an **air soft range** at home.

GAS POWERED AIRSOFT PISTOL

The second pistol I believe everyone should own is one of the **Ruger 22/45s**. This handgun can perform many different functions. It can be used for everything from a trail gun, to a range gun, to a beginner's competition gun for rim fire events. It has a number of features that make it very valuable as an initial training gun for a new shooter. Its touch and feel are similar to many **Semiautomatic Pistols**, in particular the **1911**. Its weight is similar to that of larger caliber pistols, the grip is the same as many of the larger caliber pistols, and its front and rear sides are similar to those used on larger caliber pistols as well. And, of course, another big benefit is that the cost of ammunition is much less than that of a 9 mm or a 45 caliber pistol. I find they shoot very well and they're very accurate.

RUGER 22/45 PISTOL

And finally I believe every shooter needs what I call a range gun. And in my opinion the **Glock 17** is probably the best range gun on the market today. They're powerful enough to easily be used for self-defense, they're easily available at prices around $500, so they're not really expensive, 9 mm ammunition is fairly inexpensive, their maintenance is very simple and straightforward, and they just shoot every time you pull the trigger. When you marry the **Glock 17** with a Blackhawk Serpa holster, a good pistol belt, and a couple magazine holders, along with a half a dozen magazines -you have what I believe is nearly the perfect system to use for virtually any kind of training course you want to take.

So there you have it. These are the three guns I believe every new shooter should have in his range bag: a good quality **air soft gas-powered pistol**, a **Ruger 22/45**, and finally a Glock 17 with a total of six magazines, a **Serpa Holster**, two magazine carriers and a good pistol belt. With these tools in his range bag, a new shooter is ready to take the next step to really begin learning his shooting craft.

GLOCK 17 PISTOL

A Range Day

So you're going to the range – yippee, skippy. Why?

I'm gonna practice! Ah … it's so much clearer now … what ya gonna practice?

MMmmmm – making small groups … or adjustin' my sights … tryin' out a new gun … or some other equally vague comment . . .

So, with .45 Cal ammunition in the neighborhood of $75 a round and 9mm in the region of $.60 a round … . really, you're just makin' holes or tryin' guns? Really?

Perhaps a different approach would server you better. Rather that tell you what to do, let me describe my morning, the reason for my plan today, changes I made and the AAR to fully evaluate my range time.

My Plan: I go to the range with a plan in my mind, specific things I want to work on. Today I wanted to spend a bit of warm up time with my **Ruger .22/45** then switch to my **Glock 17** and work on marksmanship, longer range for a couple of magazines to see how I was doing there and finally to go through the drills I taught at the last course: two-hand full extension, one-hand ¾ Hip, one-hand ½ Hip, Close Hip and the Zipper.

What I did: I followed the plan, but all the way through with the **.22/45** and with nearly two hours under my belt (and the lawn waiting at home), I took a pass on the 9mm practice.

Targets: I use a variety of different targets –a half dozen 3x5 cards stapled on the cardboard, a 6 plate for the head and 8-1/2 x 11 for the body, law enforcement targets. Honestly, I'm not fond of traditional bull's-eye type targets; I've long-since stopped using them. They have a tendency to have a shooter focus on their grouping rather than the dozens of other things that are going on to make **Combat-Effective Hits**, so I let them be.

Recently I've become fond of **Law Enforcement Targets** paper targets. They have just about everything you can think of. I've settled two versions:

<u>An FBI Q Target:</u>
The cost of this target is currently $34 per 100.

And a SWAT Training Target:

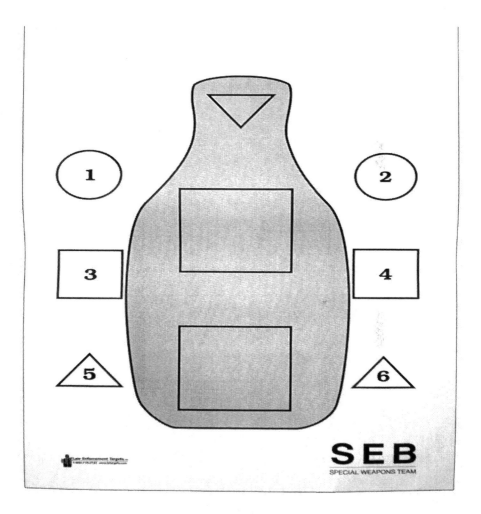

The cost for this target is currently $38 per 100.

Both targets offer the advantage of command drills, marksmanship drills and a way to evaluate **Combat-Effective Hits**. For their cost, they are well worth the extra money.

Weapons: I took my two favorite range guns – my **Glock 17** (currently my carry gun as well) and one of my **Ruger .22/45s**. I carry in a strong-side, IWB leather holster from Blackhawk. This holster will easily accommodate both of these weapons nicely. So, for all the drill work with the **.22/45**, a **Draw** from concealment with a three-four-round engagement was used.

GLOCK 17 PISTOL   RUGER 22/45 PISTOL

Yes, I know – the **Grip** is a slightly different cant and the **.22/45** uses thumb safety like on a **1911**. I accept that and train with it. It costs me nothing to flick a safety on the **Glock** and keeps that muscle memory alive for the times I carry my **1911**. Other than that the weight, fit, feel of the **Grip** are similar enough to provide solid training for the **Draw Stroke** of my **Glock 17**.

Just a quick word about **Conversion Kits** – I just don't like them. I have a couple of friends that have them for their **Glocks** and they seem to spend as much time with their pocket knives popping non-ejected casings from the chamber as they do working their training plan. My plan today for the **.22/45** ran 180 rounds without a single failure. I'll take it.

The Plan: The target today was the **SEB Silhouette** with the circles, squares and rectangles. First I wanted to warm up and work on marksmanship a bit with the six shapes. All shooting was done from the low ready, ten rounds per shape. Here are the results:

5-Triangle: 5-yards, 10 rounds, 8/10 or 80%

6-Triangle: 7-yards, 10 rounds, 8/10 or 80%

3-Square: 10-yards, 10 rounds, 9/10 or 90%

1-Circle: 10-yards, 10 rounds, 8/10 or 80%

4-Square: 50-feet, 10 rounds, 8/10 or 80%

5-Circle: 50-feet, 10 rounds, 3/10 or 30% (something about "went to shit" comes to mind…)

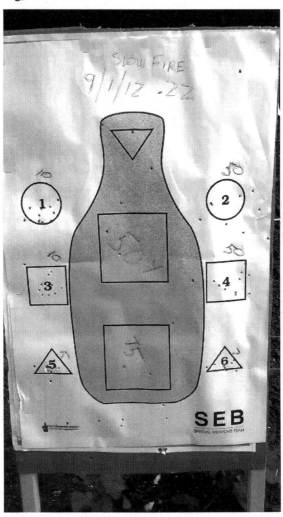

Lower Square – center-line: 75-feet, 10 rounds, 3/10 (see line above . .
. .)

Square – Center Mass 50 yards, two-hand grip, aimed fire, standing, 10
rounds, 7/10 or 70%

Not bad with going to hell at 75-feet and 50-feet on the Five-Circle. This
will give me a comparison for my next trip shooting these same drills. Is
100% possible on all shapes? Sure. But remember, defensive shooting is a
balance between speed and accuracy. If you focus so hard on 100% that your
engagement times become exceptionally long, you are teaching your body to
be slower and more accurate rather than quick and sure.

One other **Training Tool** – your **Smart Phone**. Take photos of your target
between drills (before you tape it up) so you can keep it for your records and
do an analysis similar to what I am doing here. My target, after this process
and before taping, looked like this:

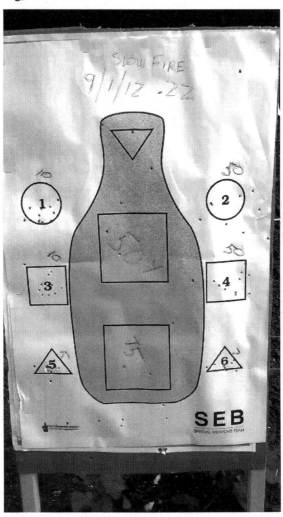

Pretty easy to see the hits, count and record them and provide a secondary way to track your progress.

From here, I moved to the shooting drills. I did six of them.

1: 21ft – 20 rounds, two-handed, full extension, top of weapon slightly lower than traditional aimed fire.

Results: 19/20 or 95%

2: 21ft – 20 rounds, one-handed, ¾ Hip

Results: 18/20 or 90%

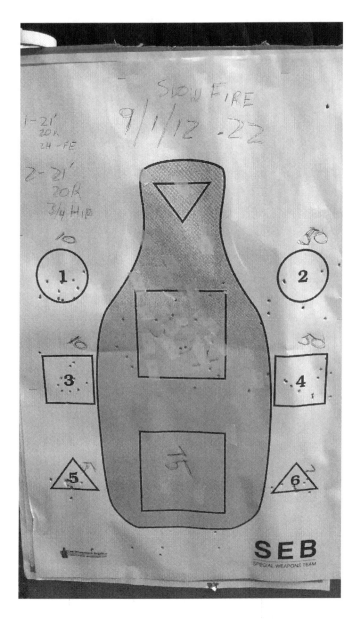

3: 21ft - 20 rounds, one-handed, ½ Hip
Results: 15/20 or 75%

Note here that for the **½ Hip** and **Close Hip** the ability to use your peripheral vision to assist in aiming your weapon diminishes – and your hit rate will suffer as well.

Simply body index is not the best aiming method in the world, and this shows it. Yet, what would happen if we would keep this type of shooting where it belongs – 15 feet or less?

5: 15ft – 20 rounds, one-handed, Close Hip
Results: 19/20 or 95%

6: 15ft – 20 rounds, one-handed, Zipper (engage at Close Hip then continue to engage as you extend to Full Extension)
Result: 18/20 or 90%

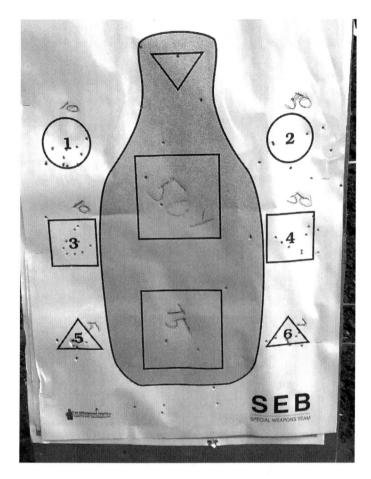

By the time I finished this set of drills, the old Pathfinder on my wrist said I had spent nearly two hours on the range. There was simply no time for a repeat performance with my **Glock 17**. The lawn was waiting, I still needed gas – my range day was over. Yet, I felt good. I was happy with the results, found some areas that always seems to need polishing and had a nice batch of data to take home and review. Not bad, not bad at all.

My suggestion to you, especially new shooters – making holes is fun; but with a little forethought, a little extra work and a little more attention, you can easily turn your drilling holes session to a solid training session that can quickly advance your skills.

Spring Training!

Opening day of the 2013 baseball season – about time! If you have followed some of my blog posts or FaceBook posts, you quickly realize it's been a very long and very chilly winter this year. And, I will confess that feet of snow and sub-zero temps have done quite a bit to keep me off the range. (Let's not even talk about the availability of ammo!)

So, while it's taken a bit of time – temps are supposed to nudge the 60s this week, so, as with the boys of summer, it's time for some spring training .

Where to start . . . where to start . . . .? Some thoughts:

The Basics:

I want to take this from a **Personal Defense** POV – things to work on to bring your skill sets up to speed if they have diminished a bit over the winter due to fewer range trips. So let's start with the basics.

Marksmanship:

As I have said before, I am fond of **Law Enforcement Targets**. In particular I like the following two:

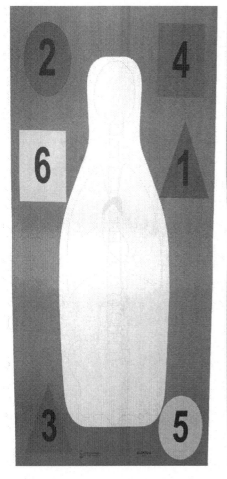 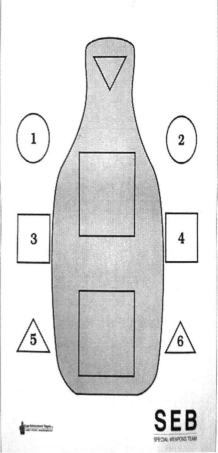

In the event you don't want to use these types of targets – a large sheet of cardboard with six-inch paper plates and/or 3x5 cards will work just as well. Number them for ease of scoring.

Both provide a range of target options as well as a good silhouette for defensive drills. I use the triangles for marksmanship drills at 3 yards, the circles for 7 yards and the squares for 10 yards or 50 feet, depending on how much I want to push myself that day.

I typically use my **.22/45** for marksmanship drills. I do not find the difference in touch and feel to be significantly different enough to warrant using higher priced ammo for these drills.

I begin at the 3-yard line and engage each triangle with 20 rounds each, slow fire. Each course of fire is shot from the **Low-Ready**. I focus on my **Stance**, **Grip**, **Sight Alignment**, **Sight Picture** and **Trigger Press**. I work on breathing through the course of fire with about a two-second pause at the bottom of my exhalation. Easy, smooth, consistent **Trigger Presses**. No need to hurry.

Just as a reminder – after a winter's slow down, take extra care with your range safety. While range work may well be a common occurrence during the warmer months – time away can diminish anyone's skills. Remember your 4 Rules and practice them diligently.

Date your target; list the caliber of handgun you are using. When you have completed each shape, score it. Use a bold marker so it's easily visible. One point for within the boundary of the target – none for any round outside. Write the score and the distance next to each shape. Start with the triangles from 3 yards, circles from 7 yards and finally the squares at 10 yards or 50 feet – your choice. 20 rounds for shape, 6 shapes . . . 120 rounds total for this portion of the exercise.

Once this is complete, all shots fired, all shapes scored – take an image of it with your cell phone. It can be a great **Training Aid** as you move through your range work. Finally, tape the target. I just use a cheap roll of ½ inch masking tape. Tape ALL holes, not just those around the shapes. When you're done with this you are ready to move to the real work.

With the rust shaken off (I do this particular warm-up for every dedicated defensive pistol range trip), it's time to move to your **Primary Defensive Weapon** – from the **Low-Ready**.

Keeping in mind the risks that arise with a timer (it can become more important to push the shot rather than making the shot), there is value in having a random tone begin each course of fire.

Again, I start at the 3-yard line with 10 rounds. From the **Low-Ready**, at the sound of the timer put 2-3 rounds in the triangle for a head shot. If you mix the round count through multiple magazines you can also add in some speed reloads as well. Clear all malfunctions as needed.

The next 10 round course of fire is from the **Low-Ready** at the 7-yard line. Use the same process and engage the square that is at center mass.

The final 10 rounds are from either the 10-yard line or the 50 foot line – your choice. Again, from the **Low Ready** – 2 or 3 rounds for each timing event. Total round count – 30 rounds.

This would complete your warm-up. Score your target as above and take an image for future reference. Then – tape your target.

Finally – you're ready for the core of your **Training** – **Defensive Engagements**. A couple of reminders: Clear your clothing. Make sure shirts/blouses are properly tucked in. Make sure the holster is clear and that you are wearing a sturdy belt designed to support a weapon. With an empty weapon, (check it THREE times), do some dry fires. Work on a clean **Grip**, **Draw**, rotation, joining, extension, **Sight Picture** and **Trigger Press**. For the 3-yard and 7-yard distances, work on a **Metal on Meat Sight Picture** – the center of the rear of your weapon in the middle of the meat of your target. Work your **Draw** until you have worked out the kinks from the winter. As for **Re-holstering** … remember … YOU HAVE ALL THE TIME IN THE WORLD TO PUT YOUR WEAPON BACK IN THE HOLSTER. Take your time.

Once this is done, step to the firing line and repeat the exercise that you did above for your **Primary Defensive Weapon** - 10 rounds on the triangle in the head from 3 yards, 10 rounds center mass from 7 yards and 10 rounds on the lower square from 10 yards. The difference this time is that each time the timer sounds you **Draw**, fire 2 or 3 rounds and then **Re-holster**. You could also mix the round count between multiple magazines to force speed reloads. Finally – clear malfunctions as they occur. Total round count – 30 rounds.

When you're finished, score your target and take your final image.

Before you leave – clean up. Check your weapon – THREE TIMES – make sure the magazine is out, chamber is clear and all magazines are empty. Police up your target and brass – as the scouts always say, leave the site cleaner than when you found it .

Obviously, these are my thoughts and this accurately describes a typical range session for me. Once the rust is off, I will go straight from the .22 marksmanship drills to the 60 rounds – from a holster **Draw**, skipping the **Low-Ready** work with my **Primary Defensive Weapon**.

Bottom line – you must work on your skill set. Range time is simply a necessity, and this is but one option.

Seconds Count … seconds count …

One of the scenarios I use in my Defensive Pistol Course is the Big Box Store Parking Lot. I don't mean to pick on the Big Box Store – nor do I mean to imply that their security is worse than anyone else's or that they are dangerous places. What I do mean to imply is that such places are rich with prey for a predator intent on an easy victim.

Such parking lots provide a broad range of opportunities to stalk a victim, to conceal their approach and to provide a moment when a predator can attack quickly and easily …

Seconds count … .

Tenths of Seconds Count …

During an attack like this, distance equals time. The more the distance between you and the predator, the greater the chance you go home that evening. The closer the distance, the closer you are to a Ziploc. Really, it's that simple. Earlier I referenced what appears to be the source for the 21 feet – two-seconds rule of thumb. If the predator is within 21 feet, you have two seconds to respond to defend yourself. Can you **Draw-Aim-Fire** in that amount of time? What can you do, as the prey, to either shave time from your **D.A.F. Response**? Let's chat about that a bit.

Obviously, your very first choice would be to not find yourself under such an attack. Beef up your **Scan and Assess Process**, pay attention, park close to the doors, park in well lit areas, go when the store is busy and during the day if possible. Listen to your gut … if something feels off, IT IS! Return to the store, walk toward other people, put your hand on your weapon … **MOVE, DO SOMETHING, GET OFF THE DIME, THE X , YOUR ASS.** Choice, movement, action will force a predator to react, adjust, reacquire and decide whether to continue the stalk and attack or to take a pass for today.

All that said, and despite your best efforts – you may well find yourself in the **Red Zone** with no choice but to fight. Now we are within the two-second window. How do you gain time (now measured in tenths of seconds) to execute your **D.A.F. Response**?

Movement: ACT FIRST! CHOOSE, MOVE, GET OFF THE X . Your best direction is at a 45 degree angle away from the predator, NOT straight back. Why? To shoot you while you are moving straight back simply means he needs to lower his weapon a tad while you retreat – no big deal.

If you back-peddle away, you are moving while being completely blind (even though your kids are sure you have eyes in the back of your head). You can easily trip, lose your balance and end up on your ass – prey for the feast.

Moving at an angle forces the predator to continually change his sight picture. It allows you to use some peripheral vision to see where you are going. And it is much easier to be sure-footed while moving at an angle than while running backwards.

MOVE!

Draw: I did a whole chapter on **The Draw** awhile back. The biggest thing you can do to shave tenths off here is to dry fire, dry fire, dry fire … Train as you would fight – if it's winter, your practice should be in your typical winter gear. Shed the gloves, grasp and clear, **Draw** and rotate … .

And let's just stop there a bit. …

You have practiced your **Draw** – dressed appropriately – and worked out all the kinks. Shedding gloves, solid grasp and clear, smooth **Draw**, good holster, good holster placement (or other method of carry – purse, carry pocket in your coat). This training, this muscle memory, has the opportunity to buy you a couple more tenths of seconds.

Now what … is that it?

Let's look at **Aiming** for a bit.

Combat Effective Hits - Metal on Meat : Here, too, I have offered my thoughts on **Sight**. In a **Close Quarters** situation, **Metal on Meat** will get the job done! Look at the threat, put the **Metal** – the rear of your weapon's slide – in the middle of the threat's **Meat** and press the trigger. You will get enough **Combat Effective Hits** to change the threat's mind about attacking you and to make him stop threatening you.

Some cautions: I'm going to explore **Focal Point Shooting**. **Point Shooting** is probably as old as the very first firearms. My first real exposure to modern **Point Shooting** was when I took the Suarez International Point Shooting Progression course this past April of 2012. It did a great deal to marry together many techniques I have been taught over the years.

There are real limits to this type of shooting. While less that optimal for those predators moving in on you when they are beyond 21 feet, within that distance – this skill set is a life saver. And that is how I teach it and how I would encourage you to practice it. My standard distance is 15 feet. It is for **Close Quarter** battle – not long distance, aimed fire.

Fifteen feet … seconds ticking away … down to 1.5 seconds to respond … now what?

In the late 30s there was an unlikely duo working the streets of Shanghai, China - W.E. Fairbairn and E.A. Sykes. During their time together they engaged in the neighborhood of six hundred gunfights at various distances – from up-close and personal to engagements of longer distances. They trained local police forces, made recommendations of weapons as well as shooting ranges and the types of targets that should be used. As WWII grew they went their separate ways, but each undertook the training of various special operations groups for the allied forces in the use of the handgun as an effective defensive and offensive weapon. Their thoughts were captured in a book they penned entitled **Shooting to Live** . It's a short, concise and very clear text on **Close Quarter Combat** with a handgun. Buy it – read it – you will find it well worth your time.

For the purposes of this post, with a predator within the 15 foot range . . . there are three methods of engagement that are well worth talking about, practicing on the range and incorporating in your toolkit of **Close Quarter Combat: Close Hip** , **Half Hip** and **Three Quarter Hip** .

Close Hip:

While it's not a perfect photo of the position, this is the **Close Hip** position:

The one fault with this image is that obviously the weapon is NOT parallel with the ground. That said, it is a good illustration of **Close Hip** . Your garment has been cleared, your weapon drawn, your elbow locked and driven **DOWN** – rotating your weapon to a position parallel to the ground. Your forearm is tucked firmly into your side. Your weapon is snugged into your body. This position offers many benefits in a **CQC** situation. The first is speed. With your **Focal Point** on the center mass of the predator, your body indexed on the predator – at the 15 foot distance you can engage your predator fully confident that you will be able to get a **Combat-Effective Hit** that will either stop the threat, change his mind or, at the very least, buy you enough time to press off additional rounds as his approach continues.

This is also a position that provides good retention of your weapon against a predator who may see an advantage in taking your weapon to use it against you.

Half Hip:

If you have the luxury of time (threat still within 15 feet) you may begin extending your weapon toward the threat to increase accuracy and to move toward a two-handed shooting grip.

Notice that in this position my support arm is up in a defensive position; my weapon has been extended toward the threat, parallel to the ground. It is still in a position to press off additional rounds. I can begin to see it in my peripheral vision, so indexing becomes more accurate and I can make additional **Combat Effective Hits** in an attempt to terminate the attack.

Three Quarter Hip :

Fairbairen-Sykes determined that the **Three Quarter Hip** was the most common position of engagement for the majority of their gunfights.

Again, my support arm is up in a defensive position; though my weapon is not nearly fully extended, it is quite easy to use the top of the slide to index on the threat, making **Combat Effective Hits** a much easier task. A caution, though – as you move from **Close Hip** to **Half Hip** to **Three Quarter Hip** – retention becomes more and more of an issue. **PAY ATTENTION!** Your weapon should be pried from your dead, still warm hands – not handed over as a gift.

One other thing to note – as you drive towards the **Focal Point** you are holding on the predator's center mass. You will notice that the barrel of your weapon rises as your arm extends. By simply staying focusing on the predator's center mass and pressing off rounds as you extend, you will stitch a line of damage up the predator's body. Suarez (and Roger Phelps, the instructor, in particular) calls this the Zipper – it's a good name.

By incorporating these three shooting positions into your tool kit you provide yourself the ability to get the first hit in this age-old dual between predator and prey. With a day's instruction on the range, virtually all the folks were able to make solid, **Combat-Effective Hits** in the two second range. They trimmed many tenths of seconds off their engagement times when they set aside the standard two-handed, sight alignment, sight picture shot and worked on the Fairbairn-Sykes positions.

I would encourage you to work with this method, try it out, consider the **Suarez Point Shooting Progression** course to refine it – Roger Phelps does a great job!

Seconds Count … .

Tenths of Seconds Count …

It's your job to be ready …

To stop the threat BEFORE you become a victim. . . .

Fastest through The Loop Wins

There was a puzzle contained in the tally of air-combat stats during the Korean War that a young Air Force pilot by the name of **John Boyd** was curious about. Even though the **MIG-15** and the **F-86** were very similar (though the MIG-15 could turn faster, the F-86 flew faster), the F-86 won 90% of the dogfights. Why? As he dug into the airframes he noticed one striking difference – the MIG had manual flight controls but the F-86 had hydraulic-assisted flight controls. Over the course of the dogfight, the MIG pilot became fatigued much quicker because of his physical input into controlling his aircraft. A fatigued pilot is a dead pilot. The F-86 pilot could simply perform more maneuvers in the same amount of time because the hydraulics greatly reduced the fatigue factor. The MIG pilot was forced to react to the F-86 rather than controlling the engagement, allowing F-86 pilots to win 90% of their engagements.

The mechanics of the F-86 allowed the pilot to take advantages of a design flaw of the MIG by applying a warrior's mindset much more quickly. A warrior – even in the heat of battle – will remain conscious of what is occurring around him. He will continually dial this into his situation – location, round-count, location of fire, deployment of his comrades, weapons being employed. A warrior will then choose a method of battle to fit this new or changed or changing situation. This may be conscious or simply a reaction based on years of combat and training. Finally – a warrior acts – decisively, furiously, with all appropriate force. After his attack (or counter attack) … he will repeat this process again; he will see what's happening around him, he will see its effect on him, he will pick an appropriate response and he will do it. And he will do this again, and again, and again until he wins the engagement or is carried from the battlefield.

He will **Observe** his surroundings and the battle. He will **Orient** these results with his current situation. He will **Decide** on his next move. And, he will **Act**.

John Boyd took the spirit of the warrior, the observations of a fighter pilot and the stubbornness of a man possessed of a passion to be the absolute best at his craft and created a battlefield philosophy that has come to be known by its acronym – the **O.O.D.A. Loop.**

Fine, fine – how the heck does a warrior's response in combat apply to little old me walking down the street with a couple of prospective bad guys tagging along a half block behind me? Let's spend a bit of time on each element first, then add them to your survival skills.

Observe: Fighter pilots in particular – though virtually any pilot – develop a swivel neck very early in their careers. If you don't see a threat – you die. Simple, really. In the early days of dogfight-craft, pilots had open cockpits and silk scarves around their necks to stave off massive chafing from turning their heads constantly to scan for threats. Heck, even in my days in Vietnam I knew pilots who had a fondness for something soft around their necks to reduce their wear and tear. The other thing that has stuck around – the open cockpit. Obviously today's pilots aren't exposed to the force of a Mach-two wind, yet the canopies on virtually all top-end fighters are bubble canopies. They provide a maximum viewing area to insure the pilot has the best chance to catch an on-coming threat.

You need to develop a swivel neck as well. Put the phone down (get an ear piece instead), keep your eyes up, scan the area around you. Look who is around the cars in the parking lot, or standing in the doorway, or coming toward you down the sidewalk, or sitting in a car on your street ... I'm not asking you to be a paranoid freak, (well . . . maybe a little paranoid), but I am asking you to be **Observant** of your surroundings. Pay attention.

Orient: Orientation is a little simpler for a fighter pilot. A scan of the boards will tell him where he is, what his weapons load is, how much fuel he has and the location of a suspect aircraft or a missile threat or a good guy who needs help. . . . Because of his/her current mission, the focus is much narrower than it is for you walking down the street.

Through your **Observations** you notice what you think is a developing threat. It is time to **Orient** yourself. Where are your exits? Are there friendly areas nearby that you could move towards? Do you have a companion along whom you need to share your concerns with? Where are your weapons – knife, flashlight, pepper spray, gun, spare ammunition? What are you wearing – can you run easily or will you need to shuck your shoes for better footing? Do you have your kids along? Have you gamed such a situation with them so they know how to react? Will they obey your commands?

Such thoughts are why I use the phrase, "You have all the time in the world now to plan or hit the range or prepare in some other way for this exact instant. Use it."

Decide: For a pilot on a combat mission, the decision to engage and kill an enemy aircraft or enemy tanks or enemy missile platforms or enemy troops can be much easier than your deciding to engage the two suspected bad guys tagging along a half a block behind.

The pilot who overthinks his **Decision** is a dead pilot. If you get stuck in the **Observe/Orient cycle** and fail to move on, you, too could well end up in a Ziploc.

Decide on a specific course of action at that specific instant. **Decide** to move into a building, between a pair of cars, towards a group of people – make a **Decision**.

Act: MOVE! **Act** out your **Decision**!

And then … immediately enter the **Loop** again. Perhaps you determine there is nothing to worry about – the threat you saw was simply two buds bar hoppin'. Or perhaps your fears are confirmed and their steps continue to follow yours.

If that is the case, you can move much more quickly to the **Decide** step because much has already been confirmed by their reaction to your first action. This is getting inside the **Loop** – you are forcing them to react to you rather than being at their mercy. **Act** first – make them respond to you – stay **Focused** – remain aware of your surroundings.

And, if need be – engage them directly. If you cannot escape to safety, lying to yourself that surely this is not happening will insure you have a very bad day. Engagement is always the option of last resort, for you are not a combat pilot on a mission deep in enemy territory. Yet, you HAVE become a warrior. You are well conditioned, you are skilled in the use of your defensive weapons (everything from a tactical pen to a flashlight or the weapon on your hip or in your purse). If your very life – or the life of your spouse or child or friend – in is in mortal danger, your weapons are free . Act with violence, with overwhelming force, with deadly accuracy.

The fastest through the **Loop** wins …

. . . it's that simple …

It's better to be quick than to be dead.

Training matters – work on your skills each and every day, without fail.

Oh, if I haven't said it enough …

WEAR YOUR DAMN GUN!

You are a TARGET!

Make no mistake, when you walk down a street, across a parking lot, take out the trash or drop your kids off at school – you are a target. Obviously the other ingredient to make this fact a problem for you is some bad guy out there looking for a soft target – you. You may go your entire life and never have these two elements meet. Or, it may happen tonight when you take the garbage out. So how do you reduce the threat in the event these two elements do, indeed, join? It's called **Situational Awareness**. Let's explore what that means for just a bit.

The individual who really introduced America to modern-day gun fighting is Lt. Col. Jeff Cooper. In the mid-70s he started the American Pistol Institute to teach his skills to military, law enforcement and civilian shooters. This grew into the world-famous Gunsite Training Center . One of his most famous contributions to shooters is the **Cooper Color Code**. Do some more reading on your own about this, but I will do a short breakdown here:

Condition White: You are unaware and unprepared. Here the only thing that will save you is plain dumb luck.

Condition Yellow: You are Relaxed and Alert. There is no specific threat that is obvious, but you are scanning your surroundings, continually updating your **Situational Awareness** level.

Condition Orange: You have identified a specific threat. Your gut tells you something is off. It may be an individual or individuals who seem to be paying undue attention to you. You may notice you are being followed while you are walking or driving. You begin to remind yourself where your weapon is, how to access it, begin evaluation exit routes, types of cover.

Condition Red: You fight. All your lines have been crossed; you believe you are in mortal danger – if you don't fight, you will die. It is an **E.T.** – an **Existential Threat**.

I have adopted this color code for a target – with YOU in the middle. It looks like this:

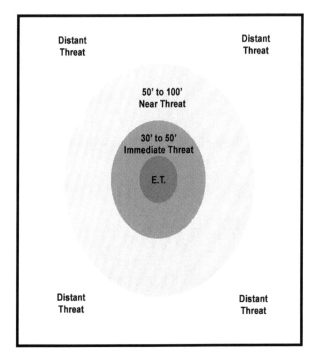

Distant Threat - +100 Feet

You're aware, you identify a possible **Threat**. It's time to move toward safety, evaluate possible scenarios and your probable **Action**.

Near Threat - +50 Feet

The probable **Threat** has identified you as a **Target**. It becomes more obvious that he is moving toward you. His manner is more aggressive. His gaze is more intense. You prepare for flight or engagement.

Immediate Threat - +30 Feet

You are an obvious **Target**. Your hand is on your weapon. Loudly announce you are armed and you will engage him if necessary. Draw and present when he is within 25 Feet. (Note: at this distance you have less than two seconds to **Draw** and acquire the threat.) Engage if required.

Existential Threat - 5 Feet or Less

This is an **Immediate Threat** that has given you no warning. It came from around a corner, was waiting for you when you opened your door. It completely bypasses all preceding levels.

Immediately cover your face and head with your forearms. Move into attacker. Pivot your dominant side away. Take your support side arm and secure your attacker's arm that is nearest to your weapon. Draw weapon, index and engage.

From a practical point of view, a person simply cannot maintain **Condition Orange** – the level of awareness displayed at the **Immediate Threat** ring for a long period of time. The reality is that you're NOT under **Direct Threat** for most of your life. Not everyone is your enemy – yet they may be. Perhaps General Mattis says it best: "Be polite, be professional, but have a plan to kill everybody you meet." (Check out famous Mattisisms just for fun.) Conversely, if you plug in your iPod ear buds and walk on down a crowded street, you simply scream, "Pick me, pick me!"

Condition Yellow – that's used in the **Near Threat** region of your target – it's what I would encourage you to work toward. At this level you are not paranoid, not amped up, not on edge for the whole day, you are simply more aware of your surroundings, the people around you and the vehicles in front of and behind you. This is also a great time to gameplay. What would you do, right now, if you identified a **Threat**? Where would you go? What cover is available? What are your escape routes? Can you get to your weapon? It's the perfect time to work on your preparedness while not working yourself into a state of mental exhaustion.

One other thing to notice about the **Target** – it covers a full 360 degrees. An attack on you can come from any direction. Get used to looking all around you. Use your car's mirrors, use reflections in windows, swivel your head around, don't take the same routes, don't keep the exact time table (you

ALWAYS take the trash out each morning at 6:30 AM). Change things up, take different routes home, walk a different path. I know this is all common sense. The trick is to – CHANGE YOUR LIFE STYLE. Be proactive. Refuse to be a **Target** each and every day of your life.

Support Hand Dexterity Drills

How's that for a fancy title? Brings to mind the wizardry of speed drills, speed reloads, tactical reloads – mags flyin', dump pouches bein' filled – the smell of burnt gun powder in the air ... .. MMMmmmmmmm, not so much.

I'm working on an overdue home project – the reinsulating of the ceiling in our two-stall garage. It sits below our bedrooms and, after thirty years, we yanked out all the old stuff, and installed new stuff ... except ... for the portion under our bedroom. With temps periodically slipping into the single digits at night, I was encouraged by my lovely and loving wife to get off my butt and keep her feet warm!

So, the other evening, as I am working my way through four foot sections of 9 batting, stuffing it between the floor joists and stapling the edges of the paper barriers together – I am artfully balanced on a short stepladder, half bent backwards, with a hand-powered staple gun driving ½ inch staples through the paper overlaps into said floor joists. This was made more challenging because I was attempting to do all the work with my **Dominant Hand**, rather than using both **Dominant** and **Support Hands**, depending on which could get into position easier. It occurred to me the lengths we will go to, to use our **Dominant Hand** when it may well be physically easier to us our **Support Hand**.

There's been lots of hub-bub about moving from words like "strong hand" and "weak hand" to "**Dominant Hand**" and "**Support Hand**" over the past few years. A bit of a to –maaaaa – toe / ta – may – toe issue to me, yet there is a grain of truth in it.

I am a strongly **Right Hand/Right Eye-Dominant** person; and, as can be evidenced by my efforts recounted above, I will quickly contort my body just so I can use my right hand. Honestly, that's a silly choice – and one I would suggest you look at as well.

Getting back to gun fighting, (what, you didn't know that's what we're talking about?), consistent and dependable weapons manipulation, magazine reloads, speed-loader reloads are all dependent on your ability to use your **Support Hand**. This is a skill that can be practiced on a daily basis, not just on the range swapping mags in and out.

Some examples:

Open your locks with your **Support Hand**. Find your keys, put the key into the lock and open the door – all with your **Support Hand**.

188

Standing at the range (cooking that is) getting supper ready? Switch hands and do all the mixing, stirring, flipping with your **Support Hand**.

Making a cell/phone call? Reach for your phone, open, dial, answer, send a text – all with your **Support Hand**.

Doing maintenance around the home? Switch hands and use your **Support Side** – even if it takes much longer.

Cleaning your weapons? Again, switch hands and use your **Support Hand** to do the work.

Loading magazines? Switch hands.

Use a computer? Use your **Support Hand** as your mouse hand.

What's the point of this? In a gunfight, your survival depends on your body's doing what you ask it to. Nothing is more devastating than hearing a click and muffing the reload. Or feeling a shooting pain in your **Dominant Shoulder** and realizing you are worthless with your **Support Side Hand**. Any **Support Hand Dexterity Drills** you can do – be they unlocking a door or sending a text or off-hand shooting – will help teach your body a skill set that may one day save your life.

Training doesn't just happen at the range ...

It can happen anywhere you use your hands . . . .

The art of staying alive – shoot your carry weapon!

A person who has chosen to carry a weapon for personal defense has entrusted their life to that weapon. Of course, there is the skill set to learn and integrate into your mind, body and muscles. There are the tactics to learn, the art of concealed carry, the use of cover and concealment, the integration of the Cooper's Condition Codes – and myriad other details we all strive to make seamless if/when we are presented with a life or death situation. Surely we all spend hours on the range practicing and enhancing the most basic of these skills – our marksmanship.

Yet, there is a single bottleneck that, in the shortest of seconds, can simply cast all our efforts to the wind: a weapons failure.

No, no – not a misfire, hang fire, failure to feed or a double feed (the fab four). We can train for those, account for those, and on a lucky day we can survive the seconds they would add to putting down the **Threat** that is barreling at us intent on ending our life.

What I mean is that sickening, gut wrenching feeling when you press the trigger and … … ... nothing. Zilch, zip, nada. You are about to die.

So let's chat about this a bit. Full disclosure – this has never happened to me in an actual moment of engagement. I have always felt a satisfying crack from my weapon at those moments – or have been able to clear my weapon quickly enough that it did not affect the outcome. My discomfort came on the range this weekend during our very first steel shoot – and momentarily left me a bit unsettled. Just a bit more disclosure – in my forty+ years of shooting, I have actually never experienced a total weapons failure. Ever. I have had the fab four. I have had ejector failures, failures of my sights, failures of ammunition – but never a weapon that literally died in my hands. To add a bit to my discomfort – it's my **Carry Weapon**.

We had our steel shoot this weekend. It was just an intro to the whole sport. Two stages were set – Pendulum and Accelerator, the range brief was given, timers posted and off we went. No scores this weekend – (yeah, right, ok, no written scores – just a few braggin' rights) – just introducing our members to the mechanics of steel shooting. I shot one of my **.22/45s**, my **Glock 17**, my **Springfield 1911** and my **LC9** (my **Carry Weapon**). All worked without fail until I got to the weapon I carry every single day to protect my life, the tool at the end of all the training which needs to go bang each and every time. And … it died, quit, failed, took a dirt nap!

I shoot this weapon frequently – on every range trip, in every type of weather I'm willing to shoot in. I have had it for a year and have not had a single failure of any kind – including the fab four. In fact, the night before I put a 9mm LaserLyte round in the chamber and used it for dry fire practice without incident.

So, I empty the **LC9** of my Hornady Critical Defense rounds, reload with standard 115 grain FMJ rounds and step to the firing line. The timer gives the commands to load and make ready, confirms that the shooter is ready, has me stand by and at the beep I engage the first plate. I press the trigger, and press the trigger, and press the trigger (the **LC9** has a horrendously long trigger press normally) and press the trigger, and press the trigger until I am at the very rear of the trigger guard area. I press just a bit harder and a second later – BANG! That was weird, must be the round. I move to engage the second plate – only to have the above process repeated yet again, and again, and again – as the thirty-second Par Time sounds. I unload and show clear, step to the shooters' table – and mentally do an OH CRAP .

A couple of things pop through my mind. My **LC9** is dead. Kinda hacks me off – only a year old, surely under 1,000 rounds through it (I usually shoot 2-3 magazines each range trip) – what the heck is the deal? A couple rounds of dry fire confirm that the trigger mechanism is definitely toast – and a Google search confirms I am not the only one who has experienced this problem. So, I will get an RMA from **Ruger** and send my **LC9** off for repairs.

However, the bigger OH CRAP came at the moment of failure and looking over my shoulder through the next couple of rounds. When I shoot on the range I never poke holes or hit plates – ever. I have always practiced with the intent of putting down a **Threat**. Always. So imagine my discomfort when I engaged a **Threat** that was within thirty feet while experiencing a total weapon failure. I did exactly what I chide some other folks for - I tried to fix the problem while engaging the **Threat**. I stared in disbelief at the weapon in my hand and allowed the frustration and confusion of the moment to overcome my actual need to get back on the true task at hand – defending my life. Had it been real world – my chances of survival would have diminished because of the game my head was playing – reacting to the weapon rather than the **Threat**.

So, a couple of lessons learned:

1: Shoot your **Carry Weapon** as frequently as you shoot all others. Perhaps not as many rounds, but at least as many times.

2: Practice using the other defensive weapons you carry on you person – a knife, tactical pen, defensive flashlight, hand to hand skills – your weapon may not go bang when you need it to.

3: Treat every range trip seriously. If you are just putting holes through paper – step up your game and broaden your weapons practice to include everything in your EDC.

So, today I am back to my **Glock 17** and am playing with a new drill structure to integrate alternate weapons into my training.

And … I am trying to set aside the disquiet nibbling at the back of my neck.

CHAPTER 7 – SO YOU WANT TO BUY A GUN...
NOW WHAT?

YOU HAVE REACHED A DECISION: YOU WANT to buy a hand gun. There are many reasons to purchase a gun, target shooting, plinking, hunting, competitive shooting or, perhaps it's for **Personal Defense**.

Since **Personal Defense** is the focus of much of my course work; that is where I am going to focus my attention. And, since many of the folks I train are first-time gun owners, that is who I am going to focus on.

So, you are about to purchase your first hand gun and your purpose is for **Personal Defense** . . . now what?

How much gun do you need? The movies have taught us about deadly encounters resulting in gunfights that last for tens of minutes and require multiple reloads, all while winding through a house or forest or parking garage. Reality is somewhat different. Most gunfights take place within 21 feet. The majority of those follow **the Rule of Three** – three seconds, three rounds, three yards.

These facts move our selection of a **Personal Defense Weapon** to something that is easily drawn, reliable, simple to use and with enough stopping power to put your **Threat** down quickly.

The decision generally lies between a **Double Action Revolver** and a **Semi-Automatic Pistol**. Both have their advantages and disadvantages. Let's chat about **Double Action Revolvers** first.

Double Action Revolvers

With a **Double Action Revolver**, the trigger performs three tasks: rotating the cylinder, cocking the hammer and finally releasing the hammer to discharge your weapon. Most hold six rounds – double the amount required for the **Rule of Three** .

Operation is very simple - point and pull the trigger. If it doesn't go bang, pull the trigger again. Repeat until the **Threat** is down or your weapon is empty. Time on the range practicing shooting drills will insure the former happens first.

This ease of use is what makes the **Double Action Revolver** a natural selection for a first-time gun owner. Whether you are a man or woman, the primary concern if you are called upon to use your weapon is to be able to easily get rounds on target, and a **Revolver** makes this as simple as possible. There is an added advantage to a **Double Action Revolver** in that you don't need to work any other parts of your weapon other than the trigger. There is no slide to rack, no magazine to insert, no hammer to pull back – just point and pull the trigger.

RUGER LCR

My favorite revolver is the **Ruger LCR**. This family of **Light Compact Revolvers** provides a selection of **.38 Special** and **.357 Magnum** weapons that are small, light and easily concealed. They also have the added advantage of an internal hammer to reduce the possibility of the weapon's catching on something while you are drawing it. For a first-time shooter, I recommend this **Double Action Revolver** over all others on the market today.

Semi-Automatic Pistol

Your other choice is the **Semi-Automatic Pistol**. Weapon selection here revolves much more around size, weight, caliber and capacity. In keeping with the **Rule of Three**, any **Semi-Automatic Pistol** that provides at least six rounds is more than capable of filling a **Personal Defensive** purpose. However, due to a higher possibility of malfunction with the **Semi-Automatic**

Pistol, a second magazine is a must, allowing you to quickly eject a malfunctioning magazine and replace it with a new one.

The most popular caliber for a **Semi-Automatic Pistol** is 9 mm. While this may be considered by some as being bit light, proper ammunition selection (we'll talk about that in a bit) can overcome this caliber's shortcomings in the knockdown power area.

The biggest difference in operation between the **Double Action Revolver** and the **Semi-Automatic Pistol** is the use of an ejectable magazine and a more involved clearing process in the event of a malfunction. While you need simply keep pulling the trigger with a **Double Action Revolver**, a **Semi-Automatic Pistol** requires the learning and muscle memorization of the standard slap, rack and shoot clearing process. While not difficult, the time required to perform this process wastes precious seconds when in a gunfight with your life in the balance.

GLOCK 17 SEMI-AUTOMATIC PISTOL

On the plus side, **Semi-Automatic Pistols** have a tendency to be slimmer and more easily concealed. Even .45 caliber **Pistols** can be fairly petite. My favorite **Semi-Automatic Pistol** is the **Glock 17**. It has a capacity of 17 rounds in the magazine and one in the chamber – 17 + 1. A second magazine gives me an additional 17 rounds just in case the firefight is extended or my first magazine fails. While this has been my favorite, there are a number of other good choices for a concealed carry .45 and 9mm **Semi-Automatic Pistols** as well.

So – when exactly do I draw my gun?

I was looking at a gentleman a few years older than I and in his first weapons class. In fact he had only run a couple magazines through his new handgun – a Springfield XDM 9mm. We were discussing various scenarios

RUGER LC9 SEMI-AUTOMATIC PISTOL

for encounters where an individual could feel threatened. And that's when the question came up: So – when exactly do I draw my gun?

Just to be clear – I am not a lawyer, nor do I play one on TV. I am not in law enforcement. I have no legal training. I have done my best to truly understand all the laws pertaining to carrying a weapon in Iowa and believe I have a firm understanding of them. Finally, I have taken live fire with a clear intention that I was not supposed to walk away from the encounter. Yet, those experiences were during my military days with Rules of Engagement that bear no resemblance to the US legal system. That said, here was my explanation:

In an earlier chapter – **You Are A TARGET!** – I approached parts of this topic from a **Situational Awareness** point-of-view. How you evaluate your ever-changing environment as you move through the streets of modern day society. However, I want to address the actual drawing of your weapon in your own defense and some broader issues that arise around that.

As a CCW permit holder, you will be held to a much higher standard of behavior in the event you have your weapon on you and you get into a situation that deteriorates to the point where you need to defend yourself. The best way to avoid a gunfight is to leave and not have one. There are particular actions that you will be evaluated by in the aftermath of a shooting.

Incitement: *to move to action: stir up; spur on : urge on*

You're walking down the street with your girlfriend. A fellow standing on the corner does a wolf whistle and makes some comment you feel is inappropriate. You're carrying – feeling a little extra tough because of it – so you confront the fellow and tell him what an ass he is. At that instant YOU have

Incited an escalation of the encounter. That little extra bit of testosterone you're carrying has seriously clouded your judgment. If things progress from this point to where you take that fellow's life – even to defend yourself – things will not go well for you.

Escalation: *to increase in extent, volume, number, amount, intensity, or scope*

You find yourself in an argument with an individual. Words are flying back and forth and you find yourself becoming more and more angry. Suddenly, you cross a boundary where – right or wrong – you are going to win this argument. When the smart thing to do would be to simply say something like: "Hey, ya know what, this is simply not worth arguing about, I'm going to just let it go and leave" – you double down. Again, that chunk of steel under your clothing makes you feel that you can ultimately win this argument – so you push your point . . . build the anger . . . push your point . . . build the anger ... . until there is a body on the ground and a gun in your hand. Things are not going to go well for you.

Under the influence: *you're drunk*

You're at a bar, you are carrying (BTW – this is profoundly stupid – do not carry a weapon into a bar – EVER) and you have let three or four too many drinks slide through your lips. During a game of pool your opponent cheats, (at least in your drunken state you think he cheated), an argument ensues and suddenly you feel threatened. Maybe he lifts a pool cue to take a swing at you – and again there is a dead body at your feet and a smoking gun in your hand. Things are not going to go well for you.

Brandish: *to shake or wave (as a weapon) menacingly*

True story from our region – names and places purposely left out. A lady is in the parking lot of a fast food restaurant. She is getting out of her car and a person accidentally backs into her car. She asks him to stay while she calls the police and he decides it's a good time to boogie. Her solution? She whips out her brand new revolver from her purse and holds him at gunpoint until the police arrive. Things did not go well for her.

Another example – you're in a store, in an impossibly long line, and the person in front of you is being an ass. Stupidly, you ask him to just relax, you tell him things will eventually work his way through the incredibly long line. The person truly is an ass and threatens to pound your butt into the ground. Rather than leaving, you make an equally stupid remark like: "Careful, bud,

I got a gun!" as you sweep back the corner of your concealment garment just to prove your point. You have now **Brandished** your weapon and made a **Direct Threat** on the person. Things will not go well for you.

OK, OK, OK – so when do I draw my weapon then? When I'm bleeding on the floor?

The way I explain it (again – not a lawyer, not a LEO) is that if you feel like you are in mortal danger you are (again – in MY opinion) justified in drawing your weapon, announcing to your **Threat** that you will shoot him if he continues to advance on you and then – and only then – if he continues his advance, engage him to stop the **Threat.** Obviously that does not include the **Existential Threat** that appears virtually instantly (from around a corner, behind a door, between two cars) where you simply have time to react. In that case, react – defend yourself – and then call the police and wait for them.

What is mortal danger ? It is that feeling that tells you that if you don't stop this person you will be going home to your Maker and not your family. You will die. You will be dead. Pine box city.

The after action reality? The courts will more than likely make the final decision on whether you acted appropriately. You should expect to be arrested. You should expect to have your weapon confiscated. You should expect to be questioned about the event, the steps leading up to the event, the amount of training you have had, the length of time you have carried a weapon . . . and dozens of other questions about the specifics of the event. Your answer – I thought I was going to die!

My advice for once you are past that statement? Tell them who you are, offer to answer their questions, but only in the presence of your attorney. This is your constitutional right; exercise it. I carry a card in my wallet with my attorney's personal cell phone number on it. We have discussed the possibility of a shooting event happening and we have agreed upon a plan of action. That is what I will follow – then I will answer any questions the police may have with my attorney sitting by my side.

So, bottom line – when do you draw your weapon? When you feel like you are going to die!

Otherwise, use your head and remove yourself from the situation.

CHAPTER 8 – FIRST AID

FIRST AID: *EMERGENCY CARE OR TREATMENT GIVEN TO AN ill or injured person before regular medical aid can be obtained*
I strongly believe that EVERYONE should have some type of formal First Aid training. I just see it as something a responsible person would do. Life provides an abundance of opportunities for injury – from something as simple as a small cut or blister to a compound fracture from a bike accident to a gunshot wound on the range or in a gunfight. We are human, we are flesh, blood, muscle, bone – and we can break.

I encourage you to be that person who had received enough training that he or she can respond to everything from the boo-boo to the Blow Out .

It is NOT the purpose of this chapter to provide that type of training. Please, look in your area, find out what courses are available and take one. The Red Cross is a great place to start. There are also a number of courses available to provide training for gunshot wounds as well. Find a course and take it!

The purpose of this course is to provide you a starting point for two different types of **First Aid Kits** – the **Boo-Boo Kit** and the **Blow Out Kit**. These are the **Kits** I carry with me every day – whether clipped to my range bag or behind the headrest of my Jeep, they are always within an arm's reach.

Your Boo Boo Kit

Boo-Boo: *a usually trivial injury (as a bruise or scratch)*

Simple injuries – a cut, bruise, blister, sliver, tear in your skin – are common injuries for a person who works with tools, knives or, in the case of shooters, who frequents the range – just handling our firearms. It certainly isn't uncommon for a shooter to have the web of his dominant hand torn by a handgun's slide. Or to have a finger caught in an ejection port. Or to have a thumb sliced by a magazine during a reload.

On a broader scale – if you are a hiker, camper or just doing work around the home, small injuries happen every day. For me, my lovely wife expects blood to be drawn during each and every DIY project I work on. Sadly, I mimic Tim the Tool Man all too well. The good news – I have a **Boo-Boo Kit** at hand. The bad news … I rotate stock much too often.

So, what's in it? Well, here is a look-see into my **Kit**:

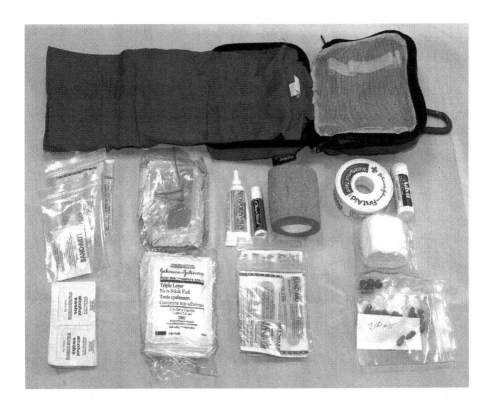

I've used a 5 x7 tri-fold pouch – this pouch actually – for over ten years. Each column shows what fits into the pouch pocket above it. So, left to right:

- Band Aides – assorted sizes
- Alcohol Wipes
- Blister Kit
- Large Gauze Pad
- Neosporin
- Chap Stick
- Elastic Bandage Wrap
- More assorted Band Aides
- First Aid Tape
- Advil
- Assorted Meds – trip dependent
- Carbineer to hook the kit to a pack, range bag, (or the headrest of my seat in my Jeep).

This is a pretty simple **Kit**. Obviously I stock what I use most – Band Aides. It is the **Kit** that rides in my Jeep, is transferred to the range bag, (along with the BOK) when I reach the range and my day pack every time I travel. Also note that I repackage everything into small Ziploc bags for some additional weather protection.

I encourage you to update the **Kit** at least once a year – or more frequently if you have a fondness for self-mutilation.

There is certainly no reason for you to pack your own – there is any number available via Amazon. However, the advantage of your own package is that you can tailor it to your own needs.

And, to go along with your **Boo-Boo Kit** – take a First Aid course to learn how to best use it. The Red Cross is a great place to start – from the basics through a Wilderness First Aid course to teach you how to handle major injuries when you're a long way from the nearest help.

Build a **Kit**. Learn how to use it.

And carry it each and every day . . . .

YOUR BLOW-OUT KIT (BOK)

There are many levels of **First Aid Kits** (IMNSHO anyway) - there's the basic level **First Aid Kit**, the **BOO-BOO Kit,** and the **Blow-Out Kit**.

Everyone – regardless whether you are a shooter, a parent or just a nice guy/gal driving down the road – should have a well-stocked **Kit** – the **First**

<u>Aid Kit</u> - that they carry with them every day. I put mine in my day bag. I update the supplies every year in May – just prior to our annual camping trip to a little island in Lake Michigan.

Everyone – especially shooters – should have a **BOO-BOO Kit** – stocked with alcohol wipes, assorted sizes of cloth band aids, antiseptic cream, medical tape – to name just a few items.

Everyone should take some type of First Aid course. The Red Cross offers a number of courses – from basic First Aid up to a multi-day wilderness First Aid course. Take one. Shooters – there are a number of companies that offer a catastrophic First aid course tailored to the types of injuries you are likely to see in a shooting incident – take one.

But, in this chapter, I want review what I believe should be in your *Holy Crap! George just got shot and he's bleeding out!* <u>Kit</u>, why it's there, where to carry it and what your priorities should be.

A **Blow-Out Kit (BOK)** is designed to handle a catastrophic event – typically a gunshot to an area of the body containing large arteries or chest wounds that would allow lungs to flood with blood or that produce sucking wounds allowing air and blood to mix in the victim's lungs, allows allowing them to collapse.

We have all learned the **ABCs** of First Aid – **Airway**, **Breathing**, **Circulation**. If the victim isn't breathing, clear his **Airway**, insure that he is **Breathing**. Check to see if he has a pulse, insuring **Circulation**. If B and C are absent, perform CPR until help arrives. (Yes, I know, new guidelines, yadda, yadda, yadda – I would perform CPR, NOT just compress the chest.)

While doing this, watch for symptoms of shock as well – when the body shuts down to protect its vital components.

However, with a catastrophic gunshot wound, a new priority appears – **Bleeding**. And, it becomes your primary concern – stop the victim's **Bleeding** before blood loss becomes so great the ABCs no longer play a part in the survival of the victim – he bleeds out and dies instead.

There are three primary arteries to be concerned with; Carotid, Brachial and Femoral. In general, the larger they are, the quicker the victim can bleed out. The Brachial and Femoral wounds can be mitigated through the use of direct pressure or a tourniquet. The Carotid becomes more difficult since it is the primary blood source for the victim's brain. Should any of these be severely damaged, death can come in mere moments.

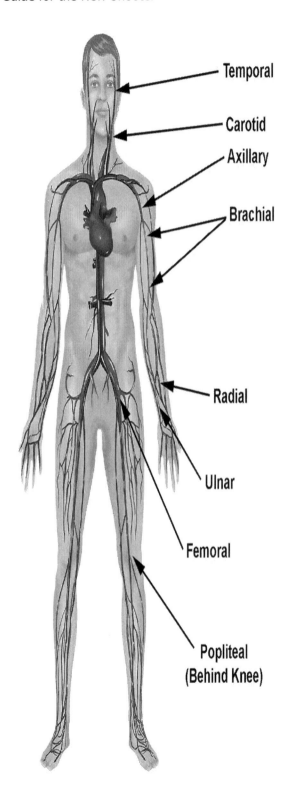

Temporal

Carotid

Axillary

Brachial

Radial

Ulnar

Femoral

Popliteal
(Behind Knee)

So what components should you have in your **Blow-Out Kit (BOK)** to help George before the EMTs arrive? I've just updated my **Kit**; let me show you what's in it and why.

Obviously, you should call 911 as soon as it's practical. Give them your name, address and what the problem is. If another shooter is available, have him call while you respond to the victim.

(NOTE: All images are linked to an Amazon source)

NON-LATEX GLOVES

A good pair of **Gloves** is important for a couple of reasons; it protects you from blood-borne pathogens (AIDS, Hepatitis are two that come to mind), it protects the victim from infection from you as well, and **Gloves** make a much better seal if needed than a bare hand. My choice comes in a nice little ten-pack from **Rescue Essentials.**

TOURNIQUET

A **Tourniquet** is a rapid fix to a big problem. Its purpose is to compress the artery, about three inches above the wound, to staunch the flow of blood. I have the **SOFTT-W Tourniquet** in my **Kit** made by **Tac Med Solutions.** It has two advantages: it does not need to be slipped over a limb but can have one end detached while you get it in place, then it's easily tightened. And the windlass is aluminum rather than plastic. That helps avoid a broken **Tourniquet** just when you need it most.

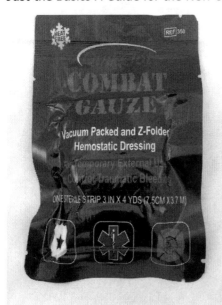

QUIKCLOT Z-FOLD COMBAT GAUZE

For large wounds that refuse to stop **Bleeding**, a **QuikClot Gauze** can save the day. In the VAST MAJORITY of cases, direct pressure and a good **Combat Dressing** will stop the **Bleeding**. For those cases where it does not, and the EMTs are not coming, **QuikClot Gauze** is a tool that can save you. I recommend **Z-Folded** because it lessens the possibility that the whole roll will simply drop out of your hand and go rolling across the ground.

Early forms of **QuikClot** had issues with excessive heat generation that could actually damage tissue. The new generation of product has reduced this risk, yet most EMTs that I know are forbidden from having this type of product in their **Kits**. Me, if I have a real problem and assistance is a long way away – I will use this, save myself or my friend, and deal with the results after help arrives.

I have **QuikClot Combat Gauze LE (Z-Folded)** sold by **Rescue Essentials.**

A good pair of **Medical Scissors** is a must. They are used primarily for removing or opening clothing to get to the wound as well as for trimming off gauze. They should be large enough to handle easily with a gloved hand and to cut and remove heavy material like jeans, tactical pants or shirts. I carry **Prestige Medical Fluoride Scissors** made by Prestige Medical.

MEDICAL SCISSORS

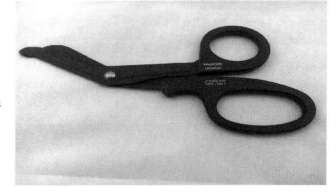

TACTICAL DRESSING

_Once the **Bleeding** is controlled, you will want to keep the wound clean and to keep a constant pressure on it. One of the best ways to do this is with a **Tactical Dressing**, and one of the best on the market is the **Israeli Dressing**. I carry the **Tactical Trauma Dressing (Israeli Bandage, 4 Inch)** by **OEM** .

There can be many instances when additional pressure or the ability to secure a limb is needed. One of the easiest ways to do this is to use an **Ace Bandage**. I got mine through Amazon directly from **ACE.**

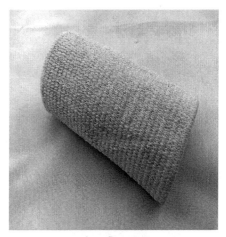

ACE BANDAGE

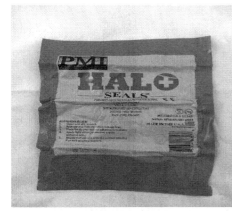

CHEST SEALS

Your lungs are the equipment your body uses to oxygenate your blood to get oxygen to your body's cells. In the event of a chest wound, your lung can begin to deflate, reducing your ability to breathe. Prior to putting a dressing over the wound, it helps to **Seal** the wound to prevent the escape of air and the collapse of your lung. A simple plastic sheet can help when held in place by a dressing. However, it can move quite easily. The use of a **Chest Seal** is much more reliable. They come in a 2-pack to cover both the entry and exit wounds. I carry the **HALO Chest Seal** sold by **Progressive Medical.**

How should I carry this stuff?

I carry my components in a small pouch that's no longer made. There are a ton of them out there, and I have no real recommendation other than it should easily hold all the components in as small a package as possible.

Obviously, if you don't carry your **BOK**, it's of little use. If you have your gun on you, your **Kit** should be reachable. This will require some playing with the packaging, but in the event you have your femoral artery shot away, the fact that your **BOK** is in your **First Aid Kit** in the trunk of your car will be of little comfort.

Finally, there are a number of fine companies that offer training in attending to catastrophic wound trauma. If you are willing to spend hundreds of dollars on training courses for using your weapons, spend a couple hundred bucks to take a combat trauma course – it could easily save your life!

When I post about having your weapon along on a daily basis, I usually say something like …

TAKE YOUR DAMN GUN!

I'll add this phrase to it . . .

AND YOUR BOK!

Every single day . . . .

206

YOUR FOUNDATION . . . .

The intent of this book was not to turn you into a gunnie, to turn you into a shooter or to even turn you into a marksman. Much of that evolution only comes through time, rounds down range and by taking course work from many different instructors.

My purpose in writing this book – and my blog – is to provide you with a **Foundation**.

Foundation: *a basis upon which something stands*
an underlying base or support

I firmly believe that every new or inexperienced shooter needs to lay a **Foundation for Growth**. They need basic knowledge, they need to know the right words, they need to have a path for growth.

That is why I wrote this book, and why I write my blog, to give new shooters a place to start. You can spend a lifetime learning new skill sets, new weapons systems, new tactics ... but everyone needs a place to start . . .

... a **Foundation**.

About the Author

Bill Keller is a twenty-one- year veteran of the US Air Force and the Iowa Air National Guard and a retired Air Force Officer. He has a military qualification as an expert with a handgun.

He is a lifelong shooter and hunter, an IDPA competitor, a member of the NRA and a certified NRA Instructor and Training Counselor for the following NRA disciplines:

- Basic Pistol

- Basic Rifle

- Basic Shotgun

- Personal Protection Inside the Home

- Personal Protection Outside the Home

- Home Firearm Safety

Bill is also a certified NRA Chief Range Safety Officer.

He is a thirty-year business owner and computer systems engineer. His business has required him to provided advanced and detailed training in a broad range of computer software and hardware. His teaching experience, military and shooting experience and business experience have now been brought to his new company – Eastern Iowa Firearms Training. His intention is to provide you with the best, most detailed and practical training available.

Made in the USA
Charleston, SC
29 August 2016